SMALL SPACE STYLE

# SMALL SPACE STYLE

## CLEVER IDEAS FOR COMPACT INTERIORS

### Sara Emslie

PHOTOGRAPHY BY
Rachel Whiting

RYLAND PETERS & SMALL
LONDON • NEW YORK

First published in 2014 as
*Beautifully Small*.
This revised edition published 2019
by Ryland Peters & Small
20–21 Jockey's Fields,
London WC1R 4BW
and
341 E 116th Street
New York, NY 10029
www.rylandpeters.com

Text copyright © Sara Emslie 2014, 2019
Design and photographs copyright
© Ryland Peters & Small 2014, 2019

10 9 8 7 6 5 4 3 2 1

ISBN 978-1-78879-090-1

A CIP record for this book
is available from the British Library.

Library of Congress CIP data has
been applied for.

Printed and bound in China

**SENIOR DESIGNER**  Toni Kay
**COMMISSIONING EDITOR**  Annabel Morgan
**LOCATION RESEARCH**  Jess Walton
**PRODUCTION MANAGER**  Gordana Simakovic
**ART DIRECTOR**  Leslie Harrington
**EDITORIAL DIRECTOR**  Julia Charles

**STYLING**  Sara Emslie
**ILLUSTRATIONS**  Selina Snow

# CONTENTS

Introduction                        6

**Elements of Design**              10
**Elements of Style**               26
**Small Spaces**                    42

   Beautifully Simple            44
   Colourfully Compact           54
   Neat and Nautical             62
   Shades of Grey                70
   A Traveller's Tale            78
   Little Boxes                  86
   Light and Bright              94
   Lofty Aspirations            102
   Wonderwall                   112
   Colourful and Creative       120
   Chic Petite                  130
   Flotsam and Jetsam           138
   A Clever Cube                148

Sources                            156
Credits                            158
Index                              159
Acknowledgments                    160

# INTRODUCTION

Small, compact, cosy or cute – no matter how you label them, homes of limited proportions can be stylish little spaces. They can be practical and purposeful too, and are firmly back on the agenda due to a number of different factors.

Social demographics have changed dramatically over the last decade or two, with more of us choosing to live individually, or as couples, and without requiring lots of surplus rooms. Property prices, particularly in the world's major cities, continue to escalate and the demand for space in large social and economic urban centres is only increasing. For students, first-time property buyers, key workers and those wanting to downsize on reaching retirement, living in a town or city with universities, multiple job opportunities, theatres, restaurants, bars and other leisure activities all close by is a hugely attractive option. Our lifestyle habits are also changing, and homes that are smaller in size can provide the perfect balance between sufficient living space and a desirable location, as well as offering more manageable household bills. Others will be drawn to the idea of a base in both town and country, with a tiny city crash-pad and a weekend country cottage, perhaps. Small spaces offer possibilities for a range of different lifestyles.

Of course, for many of us the idea of tiny interiors conjures up a romantic notion of cute cottages, caravans, sailing boats,

**OPPOSITE** Less is so often more – little corners of small spaces that are dedicated to nicely curated displays add charm and personality. A selection of decorative objects on this mantelpiece makes for a stunning vignette in a tiny living room.

**ABOVE RIGHT** Small is beautiful – a collection of tiny photographs stuck to the wall with decorative tape is a great way of adding visual interest to a tiny space and can be regularly changed for an instant refresh.

**BELOW** Creative thinking is key in a small space. In this seaside cottage, a pair of reclaimed shutters mounted on the wall makes an intriguing alternative to an artwork. They also double up as a surface on which to clip a spotlight, thus eliminating the need for a lamp table.

beach huts and the like. While these interiors, with their minuscule Alice-in-Wonderland-like-proportions, are not intended to be the backdrop for everyday life, they often contain ingenious designs that make the most of every bit of their limited space and which can act as valuable inspiration for more permanent small interiors. Think of caravans, for example, where the dining table folds down to became a double bed. Or of boats and their tiny galley kitchens, using curtains as cupboard doors and slimline space-saving plate racks to hold the tableware, plus shoebox-sized cabins with bunks custom built to slot in neatly where space is at a premium and accessed via a ladder.

To create a successful small space requires hard-working design and styling ideas, not to mention strict spatial discipline. As you will see in this book, architects and designers are well versed at squeezing space out of even the most compact interior, and a combination of creative problem solving, clever remodelling and design interventions will go a long way towards transforming tiny spaces into fully functional (and beautiful) homes. During the process of renovating my own diminutive house, the wealth of interior design ideas that I have come across over the years (both through my work as an interiors stylist and from staying in tiny holiday havens) came in particularly useful. I was aware of the spatial restrictions of compact rooms, the need for versatile, multi-functional spaces and the importance of well-thought-out storage, not to mention my desire to fully embrace my somewhat minimalist tendencies! My home became a testing ground for many of my favourite design and styling ideas, which made the most of its limited proportions, and the experience of decorating and living in my own beautifully small interior is the inspiration behind this book.

**THIS PAGE** Nautical touches work well in compact interiors, as they echo the space-saving ideas often found in ships' cabins. The combined aesthetics of a simple white wooden ladder and a rope banister that lead up to a converted attic space add bags of charm and are practical too.

# ELEMENTS
# OF DESIGN

# UNDERSTANDING
# YOUR SMALL SPACE

**ABOVE** Exposed roof structures are an excellent way of adding a sense of space to a tiny interior. The owners of this Danish summerhouse have used tongue-and-groove panelling and a skylight to fully maximize the design potential.

**ABOVE RIGHT** Attention to detail is key in the design of small spaces. Here, a tiny earthenware jug containing a single sprig of foliage beautifully emphasizes the intimate proportions of the interior.

OUR LIVING SPACES SHOULD BE INVITING, COMFORTABLE AND A JOY TO SPEND TIME IN, REGARDLESS OF THEIR SIZE. ALTHOUGH OFTEN DEEMED CRAMPED AND CONFINED, WITH SOME CLEVER PLANNING AND CONSIDERED DESIGN DETAIL, TINY INTERIORS CAN DELIVER IN TERMS OF PRACTICALITY AND STYLE. THE KEY TO CREATING A BEAUTIFULLY SMALL HOME THAT MEETS YOUR NEEDS IS TO UNDERSTAND FROM THE OUTSET HOW YOUR SPACE WORKS AS A WHOLE AND TO IDENTIFY AND CAPITALIZE ON ITS UNIQUE ATTRIBUTES.

## A SENSE OF SPACE

Before embarking on a redesign, it is worth taking a step back and looking at your space as a single architectural unit. Whatever and wherever your home, the internal space will be impacted upon by building and location factors, some of which can be modified and others that, while unchangeable, can be used in a positive way to enhance the overall sense of space.

Walk around and take note of the architectural features – the height of the ceilings in relation to the floor space and the size of

**THIS PAGE** Take some time to stand back and assess the structural and architectural merits of your space. Situated in the eaves of the building, this studio apartment fully utilizes the natural framework created by the roof beams to create a cosy sleeping nook.

the windows and door openings, and the relationship they all have with each other. Don't worry if the space is not uniform – old buildings in particular can have all sorts of quirks that only enhance the charm of an interior. Instead, assess the positives and negatives of the space. Does the interior have a sense of compact grandeur, or is it portioned up and poky?

Bear in mind too the interconnectivity of the individual rooms – is there a natural sense of flow or does it feel disjointed and awkward? Note also how the natural light works within the space. This is something that can't be altered, but identifying whether your space enjoys cool northern light or is flooded with sunlight in the morning but not later in the day will help with layout decisions and decorating choices further down the line. A thorough overview of your space will help you make the most of any design ideas you have for your tiny home.

## POSITIVE ASSETS

To identify what your small space delivers best and where its weakest points are, plot it out on a piece of paper. A sketched floor plan showing accurate measurements and indicating the positioning of doors and any restrictive structural elements such as chimney breasts or load-bearing walls is an invaluable tool that will help you get to grips with the basic layout and the natural flow between the spaces. It will enable you to determine positive features and see how you can make the most of these. It will also come in very handy later on when sourcing suitably sized furniture.

Of course, there are many ways to alter a small space, from knocking down internal walls and exposing unused loft and roof space to

extending up or out in all sorts of directions. What you can do with your space depends to a large extent on what its most defining features are, so it's worth jotting these down as well, and highlighting the ones that have the most potential. Bear in mind that this will depend to a certain extent on whether the property is a house or cottage on one or several floors, or a laterally configured studio or apartment. If you have a top-floor apartment, for example, any unused attic space could be added to the existing living space, and while some would consider this area ripe for renovation, others might decide that enclosed storage space is

**OPPOSITE** Emphasizing the natural elements of a small space can add charm and character, and offer a sense of scale. In a diminutive loft, exposed rafters and rugged brick walls have been utilized to great effect to create a bold backdrop for the industrial-style kitchen.

**ABOVE** French doors in this summerhouse make full use of the abundant natural light and the stunning sea views too.

**ABOVE LEFT** A tiny studio apartment in Stockholm has been afforded the luxury of a simple partition wall between the hallway and kitchen, cleverly designed so that it creates a sense of separation and yet not segregation.

**ABOVE RIGHT** A sliding door is the perfect way of providing a tiny bedroom with the necessary intimacy and sense of seclusion but without the door taking up valuable floor space on opening.

preferable instead. Try not to write off awkward structural or architectural features as obvious no-nos, since it's unlikely that you will be able to get rid of them anyway. Instead, think positively. In a small cottage, for example, perhaps low ceilings could be removed to expose rafters or beams, which can be stripped back and made into a design feature. Beams can also work as natural space dividers, removing the need for too many partition walls, and provide a tiny home with personality and character.

## VERTICAL LIVING VS LATERAL LIVING

Diminutive houses and cottages tend to be small due to the social and economic

constraints of earlier times, and while many modern new-builds echo their layout and scale to some extent, architecturally they are worlds apart. It is the aged charm of these period houses, with their tiny rooms, low ceilings and narrow staircases, that makes them such appealing small spaces. Often possessing minuscule proportions yet packed with character, they can make pretty little homes, sometimes with the potential for further spatial modification.

For example, moving an inconveniently positioned downstairs bathroom to an upper floor is likely to be more conducive to harmonious modern living (if the number or size of bedrooms allows it), while providing good access to any outside space that can be enjoyed will make a tiny home feel much more spacious. However, some design interventions might prove detrimental to the overall atmosphere of a small house or cottage. Central staircases and chimney breasts can sometimes be removed to create a small amount of additional space, but major structural changes such as these can completely alter the feel of an older property, so give them serious consideration before embarking on any radical alterations.

What vertical dwellings such as houses do have is the potential to extend upwards, downwards or both. Loft spaces can be converted into intimate little attic bedrooms, provided there is sufficient space for a connecting staircase, while a cellar or basement level can be damp-proofed and transformed into a cosy kitchen, indulgent bathroom or practical playroom, perhaps.

Apartments, however small and whether a modern build or a section of a period property, make great compact living spaces, as their lateral layout naturally creates a more expansive feeling of space than there actually is. They can also benefit more from a total remodelling of the interior, particularly if there is design input and expertise from an experienced architect where the greater spatial challenge may lead to more creative and workable ideas.

Lateral living has the freedom to break the mould of conventional thinking in terms of utilizing space for different functions, so 'zoning' can be factored into any redesign plans to differentiate areas for sleeping, relaxing and cooking. All sorts of mechanisms such as dividing screens, pocket sliding doors and semi-partition walls can work wonders in breaking up

a space into private areas within an otherwise open-plan interior. Clever internal cubes or pods with lower ceilings are also very successful in dividing up space without the restrictive barriers of floor-to-ceiling walls.

If an apartment is blessed with particularly high ceilings or unused roof space, then creating a mezzanine level for use as a raised sleeping or work area is a particularly effective way of creating additional room, and one that is seen in several of the case studies in this book. A mezzanine frees up valuable floor space that can be allocated to a larger living space, and creates a stunning architectural and design statement too.

**BELOW** Despite taking up a portion of floor space, the chimney breast in this house provides architectural definition and visual interest to what would otherwise be a very simple, almost boxy rectangular room. It also furnishes the room with an open fireplace, and a neat alcove ideal for a vintage shelving unit.

# PLANNING YOUR SMALL SPACE

WE ALL HAVE DIFFERENT DEMANDS FROM OUR INTERIORS, SO IT IS WORTH GIVING SERIOUS CONSIDERATION TO THE WAY YOU CHOOSE TO INHABIT YOUR SPACE. HOW SMALL A SPACE IS CONSIDERED TO BE IS RELATIVE TO THE NUMBER OF PEOPLE LIVING THERE. SPEND TIME MAKING A DETAILED PRECIS OF YOUR REQUIREMENTS AND LIFESTYLE, AND CONSIDER WHICH AREAS ARE MOST IMPORTANT TO YOU SO THAT YOU CAN MAKE THE MOST OF YOUR SPACE AND USE IT EFFECTIVELY.

A successful home is one that meets the needs of those who live in it, so think about your requirements carefully. If you work from home, then a work space that is large enough to accommodate office equipment and papers will be key. If you don't entertain or cook a great deal, then it would seem sensible to designate less space for cooking and dining and more to relaxing and lounging. A sociable couple might consider reconfiguring the layout to provide a smaller bedroom and a larger, more versatile, living, cooking and dining area. In a small cottage with two upstairs bedrooms, one could be converted into a luxurious bathroom and the room downstairs could be used for something else, such as a garden room-cum-guest bedroom. Putting some considered thought into how you want to live within your space is crucial to maximizing the potential of your home and will help you come up with clever solutions.

## WORKING TO YOUR BUDGET

Be realistic when it comes to finances and set out a budget for both the long and the short term. Major restructuring can be costly, and if that is the route you are taking, it is essential to get the planning right before embarking on decoration. You can always factor in funds for extravagant wallpapers and tiles further along, if the budget allows. Don't overlook any details at this stage. Home technology and TV and audio cabling, for example, as well as under-floor heating and lighting, can all be hidden out of sight and will benefit the aesthetic of your compact interior, thus justifying the cost.

**ABOVE** The owner of this compact Parisian studio finds that a small table and a pair of stools are sufficient for everyday meals in the open-plan kitchen space. For entertaining, he has a foldable table and chairs that are stored out of sight when not in use.

**OPPOSITE** A roomy office space can be a defining feature of an interior and is essential if you work from home. There is plenty of scope for creating one that's both practical and stylish – choose boxes and storage that are neat and tidy but attractive too, and accessorize with personal mementos and a few flowers.

**LEFT** Contrary to popular belief, cast-iron radiators are not only stylish but also practical for small interiors. Made up of connecting sections and with a range of different column widths, you can custom-make them to fit even the most awkward of spaces, such as this tiny alcove.

Architects are worth the fees they charge, as their skills can make the most of every bit of available space and they are able to obtain competitive tenders for builders and tradespeople. Before you engage the services of an architect, ask to see examples of previous designs and references. Talk through your ideas and budgetary constraints, and ask for visual sketches or computer graphics to see how their ideas might maximize your small space's potential.

If your design intentions are more about refitting or redecorating a small space to suit your own style, then bear in mind that furniture, appliances and items especially designed for small spaces can be more costly than standard-sized ones. They are usually slimmer in build and designed to fit compact spaces, so are usually worth the extra expense, particularly if they allow you to fit more units in a kitchen, for example, or squeeze a tiny en-suite bathroom into a corner of a small cottage bedroom. The quantities of decorative materials needed are likely to be relatively small, so you may be able to afford more expensive ones. When making decisions, just remember to keep your budget in mind.

**THIS PAGE** The owner of this studio apartment employed an interior architect to make the most of the tiny space. The result is this fully functioning kitchen with ample storage and a breakfast bar for entertaining.

**THIS PAGE** Stairs lead up to a platform on the top of the bathroom pod on the right and into the exposed roof space. Allowing a space between the height of the bathroom and storage pods and the rafters creates the illusion of more space.

★★★
RÉSIDENCE
DE
TOURISME
MINISTÈRE
CHARGÉ
DU TOURISME

# DESIGNING YOUR SMALL SPACE

THERE ARE ALL MANNER OF CLEVER DESIGN IDEAS THAT CAN MAKE THE MOST OF EVERY INCH OF SPACE IN A TINY HOME, AND MANY OF THEM ARE RELATIVELY SIMPLE TO IMPLEMENT AS LONG AS THEY ARE PLANNED IN ADVANCE. THINK CREATIVE, BUT THINK PRACTICAL AT THE SAME TIME.

## CREATIVE IDEAS

Dual-purpose rooms are fabulous space savers. A kitchen with room for a deep breakfast bar and stools that tuck neatly beneath might provide dining space, thus eliminating the need for a separate dining table. A tiny spare room or an unused alcove in an open-plan living space could be transformed into a compact home office with a hinged work surface that folds away after use. A vacant area under the stairs could hold closet storage with built-in shelving and hanging rail or a tiny shower room, head height depending!

Architect-designed pods and cubes are ideal for sectioning off areas such as bathrooms or bedrooms, where privacy is key. They also provide a playful sense of architectural scale within a small interior, as the pods can be as small as necessary to suit their intended purpose. For example, a tiny bedroom pod containing just the bed (with closet storage elsewhere in the space) will make the rest of the space feel proportionally larger than it is, and the bedroom intimate and cosy in comparison. The success of cubes and pods lies in their self-contained structure – they do not reach the ceiling, and the uninterrupted expanse above them creates an illusion of spaciousness. The same principle can be adopted for custom-built kitchens in small spaces, as the void of space at the top of the cabinets fools the eye into assuming that the ceiling height is higher than it actually is.

Contemporary clean-lined design works well in period properties as well as modern apartments, and architects are well versed at seamlessly stitching the two aesthetics together. The angles of old roof beams can be echoed in contemporary cupboard and staircase structures. Attention

**ABOVE** An awkwardly shaped alcove created by the slope of a mansard roof has been cleverly made into a storage-cum-display space for a collection of ceramics. Custom-built shelving allows this tiny spot to be fully utilized, and the owner's collection of decorative but functional cups and bowls in a restrained palette of neutrals and whites creates a visual display in the process.

to detail such as this affords a small space personality and a sense of grandeur, despite its compact size. Architectural ironmongery and flooring are also good ways of making a design statement in a small home where there may not be enough space for lavish decoration. Make a feature of light switches, cupboard handles and flooring, but be restrained in the amount of different styles you choose and remember that less is so often more, particularly when it comes to the design of small spaces.

## STORAGE IDEAS

As clichéd as it may sound, storage space is the final frontier for small spaces. Storage that's built in as part of the design of your space is essential, as you can never underestimate the amount you will need. Most of our possessions, while

necessary, are very ordinary and you don't want to look at them all day long, so having enough facilities for keeping them out of sight is essential. And if everything has a natural 'home', then it will make it easier for you to keep your tiny home tidy and clutter free.

Of course, the beauty of storage is that it can be incorporated into all sorts of nooks and crannies. It is worth factoring it in at the design stage, as it willl form an integral part of any building work. A mezzanine level can accommodate storage cupboards that neatly fit into the eaves of the roof, fully maximizing this unused space. Similarly, a split-level living space may have some room underneath that can hold large and bulky household items.

In a period property, you are likely to find storage already built in. Small cottages or terraced houses were often simply furnished, utilitarian spaces and it was traditional to build integrated cupboards with simple panelled doors. They are usually tucked into alcoves or above the stairwell, utilizing what would otherwise be dead space, and are often roomy enough to hold linens, towels and other household essentials.

Commissioning a carpenter to build shelving, cupboards and furniture with storage combined is a highly effective way of squeezing every little bit of available room out of a small space. Their wealth of experience of working with tight and confined spaces will be invaluable, and any extra expense

**OPPOSITE LEFT** A few simply constructed shelves transform a tiny alcove into a mini-library of paperbacks.

**OPPOSITE RIGHT** Clever storage systems are widely available and allow you to customize and fully utilize every last bit of internal cupboard space, whether it's needed for clothes storage or for office files.

**OPPOSITE BELOW LEFT** Storage solutions that also have other functions are perfect for diminutive spaces. Here, storage boxes with lids for access are also used to create an original seating area.

**RIGHT** Versatile storage is key in a small space, and this custom-built seating with drawers beneath is ideal for keeping clutter out of sight. Wicker baskets on the shelves hold smaller items and their design echoes that of the drawers, keeping the overall effect easy on the eye.

incurred is worth the final result. Wooden cabin-style beds similar in design to those on boats can fit snugly in a tiny bedroom with drawers built underneath. Benches or banquettes with storage inside can be designed to suit a particular spot. Made-to-measure shelves will transform awkwardly shaped alcoves into quirky little storage nooks, and a bookcase or storage unit can be as wide or deep as your space allows, with all sorts of space-effective configurations for paperbacks to outsize books, albums and magazines. Open-plan units can even be constructed to cover an entire wall, not only providing great storage but creating a fabulous design feature too.

ELEMENTS
OF STYLE

# GETTING STARTED

GIVE SOME CONSIDERED THOUGHT TO AESTHETICS AND PRACTICALITY, AND ANY SMALL HOME CAN BE MADE INTO A BEAUTIFUL, WELL-BALANCED LIVING SPACE. THERE ARE PLENTY OF DECORATING SOLUTIONS AND STYLE IDEAS THAT WILL HELP TO MAKE THE MOST OF A TINY INTERIOR. THE SECRET IS TO IDENTIFY THE ONES THAT ARE RIGHT FOR YOU AND YOUR OWN COMPACT HOME.

In a small space, walls, floors and even work surfaces will be in shorter supply than they would be in a larger dwelling, so in order to combine functionality and style successfully and to create a harmonious home, it is well worth spending time identifying exactly what suits your space and what doesn't. Bear in mind that while the aspect and architectural features of a space can't be altered, there are still many styling solutions that will work to great effect.

It doesn't matter what your preferred style is, whether its modern, vintage or eclectic. The key to making a small space work from a styling point of view is to shelve any preconceived ideas you may have of what a home should contain, and instead to try and enjoy the process and the challenge of creating a living space that balances practicality with style, regardless of how tiny it might be.

**RIGHT** Personal objects can be used to add visual interest to a tiny interior and don't have to take up too much valuable space. A vertical shelving unit is simple and understated, and is the perfect place for a display of artisan ceramics and sculptural pieces of pottery.

**ABOVE** Despite being a corner of an open-plan space, this pretty dining area has its own identity and sense of style. A selection of different types of seating, including a rustic wooden stool and a contemporary designer classic, adds a wealth of interest to this small space.

**THIS PAGE** A soft natural palette works well with the pared-back architectural details of this tiny space and creates a comfortable feel. A selection of shapely ceramics is softened by the linen loose cover and woollen blanket for a look that is minimal but relaxed.

**THIS PAGE** The art of display is a trick well worth learning for small-space living. Books and magazines can be piled into columns and platforms of varying heights to display other decorative objects and curios.

**RIGHT** A limited amount of decorative items doesn't have to equate to an empty or featureless interior. In this period-style coastal cottage, the striking natural hues of the bare plaster wall have been picked up and highlighted in the gold detailing on the vase and the tones of an intriguing painting that was chosen to reflect the relief detail on the original fireplace.

## MINIMALISM VS CLUTTER

Small-space living inevitably means that you will end up living with your furniture pieces and personal possessions at close quarters. While intimacy goes hand in hand with cosiness and can be a positive experience, it can also lead to clutter and claustrophobia if you fill your home with a surplus of possessions. Being tidy is very much a part of one's personal DNA – you are either naturally neat and orderly and a passionate advocate of the 'less is more' principle, or you aren't, and prefer to live with all your 'stuff' around you and to acquire new items in a magpie-like fashion.

If you have minimalist tendencies, then the pleasure that's achieved by surrounding yourself with just a few carefully chosen pieces and retaining as much empty space as possible is immense and easily attainable. If you are more of a hoarder, then it is worth subjecting yourself to the discipline of a home edit, and accepting it is something that you need to factor in every six months or so. Decluttering is as much a psychological cleansing process as it is a practical one, and (particularly if you are downsizing from a larger property) getting rid of unwanted clutter can be a very positive experience and the start of a brand new chapter in your life – out with the old and in with a new, neater and sweeter sofa, perhaps.

Small spaces do have the effect of bringing this strict discipline out in people and even former clutter collectors can become positively meticulous pretty quickly, as just a small amout of mess in a tiny room looks far more chaotic than it would if it were in a larger space. Of course, this doesn't mean that a small home requires you to forsake favourite pieces of furniture or any other treasures, but the secret is to learn to edit and balance what is right for your small home with what is right for you.

**RIGHT** Cleverly designed storage units can be custom built to any size or configuration to hold specific items such as large files or hardback books. The orderly aesthetic of regimental stacks of magazines or paperback books looks great too, and maximizes the style potential of everyday items.

# STYLE SOLUTIONS

CHOOSING A DECORATIVE STYLE IS A VERY PERSONAL EXERCISE. WHETHER YOU LOVE BRIGHT SHADES AND BOLD PATTERN OR ARE DRAWN TO MUTED TONES AND SUBTLE PRINTS, MAKING THEM WORK IN A SMALL SPACE CAN BE A CHALLENGE.

### USING COLOUR AND PATTERN

It's a fact that white and light shades will make an interior feel larger and more spacious. White reflects more light than any other colour, as well as offering an air of meditative calm that's conducive to relaxation. Fresh and clean, it also provides a great backdrop for other elements. However, in a space without much natural light, bright white can look cold and grey. The effect will depend on the natural light in an interior – cool northern light will bring out the blue tones in a colour, while sunny south-facing light will make it look warmer and yellower. If you prefer a pale backdrop, it's worth painting test swatches in a selection of off-white shades to find one that works perfectly in your interior.

At the other end of the colour spectrum, the dark and moody look also suits small spaces,

**ABOVE LEFT** A hint of pattern is often enough. Here, a contemporary geometric print cushion nicely unites the soft blocks of taupe and duck egg blue in the bed linen and the vibrant blue of the lighting wire.

**ABOVE RIGHT** Fabric lengths make pretty tablecloths. They are a good way of introducing pattern to a small dining space and a great style solution for refreshing an interior in an instant.

especially those not afforded much natural light. In such spaces, bright white can appear dingy and dull. Instead, embrace the gloom and go for powerful and glamorous dark tones to add visual drama. They particularly suit tiny rooms that want a softer, more intimate mood, such as an indulgent bathroom, as well as areas where there is very little natural light – a narrow hallway, for example. Very deep shades work wonderfully when teamed with subdued lighting to create a sumptuous and luxuriously rich feel. The secret to making these sombre shades work is to stick to a restrained palette of three or four shades from the same tonal range. As ever, it's important to do a swatch test and to view it at different times of the day to understand how natural light will affect the paint colour.

Colour can also be used to deceive the eye and give the impression of more generous proportions than exist in

**ABOVE RIGHT** Pops of vibrant colour will add a burst of postive energy to even the most diminutive of rooms. If you don't want to commit to a whole-room scheme, consider painting single pieces of furniture to create a focal point.

**RIGHT** Dark, shadowy tones can work well in small spaces, particularly those where a subdued mood is required. A restricted palette of a few complementary shades works best – in this French apartment, a strong statement has been made by using shades of grey, black and inky blue. The sober hues are complemented by boldly patterned rugs.

**THIS PAGE** Painting the floor a darker colour than the walls works wonders in rooms with compromised ceiling height. In this bedroom under the eaves, the eye is drawn to the green-painted floorboards. They cover a larger area than the ceiling, so make the room feel larger.

**OPPOSITE** White is clean, fresh and the ultimate space enhancer. This dining room-cum-work space is pristinely uniform with white walls, white blinds and even a table and benches in the same shade. To prevent the look from becoming too clinical, large paintings in soft blue add visual interest.

reality. Dark tones work well on floors, as they draw the eye down and distract from low ceilings, whereas light shades are effective on walls, where they create a feeling of expansiveness. A very light shade on the floor and a darker colour on the walls will increase the sense of floor space. Experiment to see how best you can manipulate the dimensions of your home.

Tiles, kitchen work surfaces, flooring and fabrics are all great ways of adding colour to an interior. Even accessories such as lighting, tableware or occasional furniture can be used to pack a punch. The primaries – red, blue and yellow – work well as pops of colour to energize a small space, while pastels will add a gentle, relaxed feel.

If you love pattern, then embrace it but restrict it to a few carefully chosen designs. Large patterns in small areas can add impact, but they can also dominate. They tend to work best when balanced with blocks of plain colour or pure white, which will provide the eye with a place to rest. If you are

uncertain as to whether you can live with a bold pattern, one alternative is to wallpaper the inside of a wardrobe or a fitted closet or have a patterned fabric blind in a plain white bathroom. That way you can enjoy a 'big bold pattern moment' as part of a calm interior.

If you are wary of committing to whole walls of bold pattern but don't have monastic all-white tendencies either, add touches of pattern in the form of soft furnishings. Cushions, throws, pillows and bed linen can be vehicles for bold stripes, polka dots or ditzy florals. An extra loose cover for the sofa in an alternative print can provide a welcome seasonal update. Refreshing a simply furnished small space with a change of covers, blankets or linens instantly gives it a whole new look – a dark woollen plaid in the winter months could be followed by fresh florals for the summer. And a sesasonal refresh will work well in the kitchen too – a basic all-white crockery set can be instantly updated with just a few new patterned pieces, for example.

LEFT For compact dining areas, opt for chairs that stack and store them in a corner or alcove when not in use. Paired with an extending or folding table, they are the perfect solution for those who love entertaining but have limited space.

## FURNITURE

In a small space, furniture usually works best if it is in proportion to its surroundings, particularly in living areas where several pieces will be sitting alongside each other – a bulky sofa crammed into a compact space is always going to look clumsy and cumbersome. However, in a small bedroom, creating a play on scale with a large bed – or one with a luxuriously sized headboard – is a trick that hotels use to create a feeling of luxury and comfort.

Stacking and folding furniture works wonders in tiny homes. Nesting tables that tuck under each other can be pulled out when required, while stacking dining chairs can be kept in a corner or alcove when not in use. Lightweight portable garden furniture can work well too – bistro-style folding table and chair sets have the right proportions for compact dining spaces both inside and out. A high bar table and stools will fit the smallest of eating areas, as will a hinged fold-up table attached to the wall.

Vintage pieces are often smaller in scale, so they suit compact spaces beautifully, both in terms of size and aesthetics. Flea markets and antiques fairs are ideal hunting grounds for quirky one-off pieces. Vintage wall-hung cinema seats would make a fabulous design statement in a narrow hallway, and industrial metal trolleys can be used as room dividers-cum-storage in open-plan spaces. Antique furniture also works brilliantly in today's small spaces. Most antiques were made for small-roomed period properties, so their neat and elegant designs offer both practical solutions and decorative charm. Card tables and drop-leaf tables are ideal for dining, while upholstered chairs and sofas fit snugly into small corners and under sloping roofs. Old iron bedsteads tend to be higher than their modern alternatives, offering valuable storage space underneath.

To enhance a feeling of space, source furniture and fittings made from light-reflective or transparent materials. Pieces made from glossy laminates or with mirrored finishes will maximize the available light in a space, and Perspex/plexiglass pieces seem to take up barely any room.

**OPPOSITE BELOW** Antique furniture is well suited to small spaces. This iron bedstead is a small double size – the perfect compromise between a standard single and double bed. It is also higher than its modern-day counterparts, so provides handy under-bed storage too.

**ABOVE LEFT** A bar table and a pair of stools are ideal for a compact kitchen where space is at a premium. In sleek glass and metal, they are visually space saving too and offer just enough room for two diners.

**ABOVE RIGHT** A vintage child's chair makes a cute yet practical alternative to a bedside table. It also provides a play on scale beside the full-sized bed, which is made to look larger and more luxurious by contrast.

**RIGHT** Perspex/plexiglass furniture seems almost invisible – it's ideal for a compact space, as the light flows straight through it. A stool is a highly versatile piece, as it can be used as a seat, a side table or a lamp stand.

**BELOW** A vintage metal storage unit is the ideal accompaniment to a small desk and chair in a child's bedroom, and provides plenty of useful cubbyholes for toys and books.

**OPPOSITE ABOVE LEFT** Hooks and shelves offer practical and decorative storage in this bathroom. A painted vintage shelf unit with hooks creates a display feature out of a collection of simple calico wash bags.

**OPPOSITE ABOVE RIGHT** A simple extending rail/rod and curtain have transformed a tiny alcove into a generous closet space.

The black fixings and crisp white linen curtain create a stylish and softer alternative to a conventional built-in cupboard.

**OPPOSITE BELOW LEFT** A nautical-inspired plate rack, similar in style to those found in galley kitchens on boats, offers a home to assorted tableware. Wall-mounted and slimline in design, it is perfect for a compact space.

**OPPOSITE BELOW RIGHT** Fitted units make the most of the limited space in a small kitchen. Look out for additional built-in storage solutions such as the unobtrusive plinth drawers.

## STORAGE

Simple storage solutions can offer tiny interiors an enormous amount of extra space. Take inspiration from Japanese homes, where storage is squeezed into every possible nook and cranny. Follow their example and ensure you have plenty of boxes, baskets and containers to keep your home tidy.

For items with visual appeal, hooks in all manner of different styles can create storage space on doors and walls. In a tiny bedroom, team brass hooks with pretty vintage coat hangers to provide additional clothes storage. If you are neat and tidy, you can afford to have more out on show. Fix extending rails/rods or shelving in a bedroom alcove and make a pretty display of your favourite clothing. And don't waste dead space under the bed – use large wicker baskets, colourful metal trunks or zip-up fabric containers to stash away spare bed linen and out-of-season clothes.

Follow the example of the hard-working Shakers and attach peg rails to the walls or inside cupboards. Brooms, coats, hats, baskets and chairs can all be hung from the pegs, freeing up valuable floor space. If your home doesn't have a hallway, dedicate some wall space to a set of contemporary hooks that will look like wall art when not in use. Alternatively, hang a pair of salvaged shutters or an old wooden door from the wall and add a couple of vintage hooks to create an imaginative alternative to a coat stand.

Shelving is a small-space problem solver. Get a carpenter to build bookshelves into any tiny niches or alcoves and to hang a shelf above or beside the bed if there's no space for bedside tables. High ceilings can accommodate high shelves – ideal for items that you don't need to access regularly. Add a library-style ladder that sits flush with the wall when not needed, and you'll have a design feature too.

When it comes to storage, it pays to think creatively. If you don't have the budget to have storage built in, try transforming a set of fruit crates into wall shelving, adding more crates as your needs dictate. Or invest in mesh sheeting from a DIY store and some functional hooks for space-saving wall storage in a kitchen or work space.

## DISPLAY

Wall displays can be created using anything from pictures and textiles to personal photos and mirrors, but be wary of overwhelming limited wall space with too many conflicting objects. In compact spaces, it's worth following a few simple rules.

In an open-plan interior, group pictures in different areas – each group will have its own identity, but avoid too many conflicting colours and styles, and consider some kind of linking mechanism, such as a uniform style of frame. Pictures hung in regimented rows or neat columns will bring an awkwardly shaped corner some order, while single pictures can provide a sense of subdued calm. Consider unfixed decorative elements, such as framed pictures or photographs propped casually against the wall or on a shelf to imply spontaneity. Mirrors are highly decorative and have the added benefit of bouncing light around a space. Hang them together on a wall as an alternative to paintings or prints. Keep to a similar style or shape and you can be more adventurous when it comes to positioning them on the wall.

Everyday household items can be aesthetically pleasing, so create vignettes on shelves and walls using pieces of china, glassware or utensils. Displaying such objects means you don't need to find storage space for them in a tiny kitchen. Foodstuffs such as grains and rice look effective stored in a long row of attractive glass jars, and the striking packaging of some dry goods looks great displayed on open shelves in a compact cooking space. You can adopt the same idea in a tiny bedroom, too – hang pretty bags, vintage dresses or jewellery from a bamboo ladder and free up space in the wardrobe.

Displays of personal objects add charm and personality. Keep them balanced and restrained in terms of colour and pattern. Mixing too many elements can create visual conflict and there is a fine line between interesting and eclectic, and cluttered and confused.

**OPPOSITE** A collection of abstract prints creates a striking display as well as linking the different elements of this tiny studio together. The detail in the pictures echoes the patterns of the bedspread, the vase and the pouffe.

**ABOVE RIGHT** If you have a view, use it to your best advantage – a changing seascape will grab the eye's attention far more than any piece of artwork. Here, a couple of similar visual references have been strategically placed to draw the eye towards it.

**RIGHT** In a tiny bedroom, a group of cane mirrors hangs above the bed. They work well together as a unified display, but their subtle differences offer the eye plenty of interest too.

# SMALL SPACES

**OPPOSITE** Small but perfectly formed, this dining room effortlessly combines style and functionality. Slimline bistro chairs are complemented by the fragility of the porcelain pendant light and the scattering of objects on the mantelpiece. The palette of woven wicker, rustic wood and washed linens imbues the room with serenity.

**FAR LEFT** Flowers are a fail-safe way of adding a splash of colour to a tiny room. Here, they nicely pick up on the floral print of the tablecloth.

**LEFT** Clean and unfussy, the design of the alcove shelving used throughout this house works in unison with the overall understated aesthetic.

# BEAUTIFULLY SIMPLE

A PRETTY TERRACED HOUSE LOCATED IN THE LEAFY LONDON SUBURB OF RICHMOND UPON THAMES PROVES THE THEORY THAT SMALL CAN BE VERY BEAUTIFUL INDEED. WHILE SLIGHTLY BIASED – THIS IS MY OWN HOME, AND A HUGELY PERSONAL SPACE – IN TERMS OF PRACTICAL AND AESTHETIC POTENTIAL, THIS HOUSE SHOWS THAT A COMPACT INTERIOR DOESN'T HAVE TO BE COMPROMISED BY ITS SIZE, AND HAS VERY MUCH BEEN THE INSPIRATION FOR THIS BOOK.

Built towards the end of the 19th century, my home is a classic British Victorian terraced 'two-up, two-down', designed to house workers (and their families – in the case of this house, a family with 11 children) in local industry and those who served the larger, more gentrified upper-class residences of nearby Richmond Hill. The rows of terraces here and on the adjoining roads made up a community, with corner shops and a couple of public houses. Still as thriving

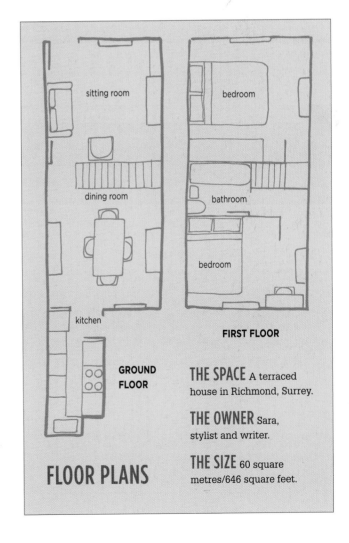

sitting room

bedroom

dining room

bathroom

bedroom

kitchen

**FIRST FLOOR**

**GROUND FLOOR**

## FLOOR PLANS

**THE SPACE** A terraced house in Richmond, Surrey.

**THE OWNER** Sara, stylist and writer.

**THE SIZE** 60 square metres/646 square feet.

**LEFT AND BELOW** Since the kitchen has limited storage, beautiful pieces of china, antique cutlery/flatware and glassware are stored on the dining-room shelves, creating an eye-catching display.

today as it was then – the pubs are there, but the corner shops have since been made into residential premises – this strong presence of community has immense pulling power for those seeking a sense of a neighbourhood rather than just property ownership. And, as areas like this are sadly becoming fewer and further between, it has been designated a conservation area/historic district, in an attempt to preserve as much of its original architecture as possible.

The vernacular of the area is, as one would expect, simple and utilitarian. The exterior of the house has a lovely, unfussy, flat-fronted, natural brick façade with original sash windows. Internally, it is equally pleasing, with a straightforward layout consisting of a symmetrical configuration of rooms dissected by a central staircase, with two rooms downstairs – living

room and dining room – and what would have been two bedrooms of exactly the same size upstairs. Fortunately, modern renovations have allowed for a portion of the back bedroom to be sectioned off and a small upstairs bathroom to be created – somewhat essential for today's living. Equally, an extension/addition at the back now houses a kitchen that leads out onto a pretty patio garden.

Each room is tiny, with the main ones measuring barely more than 3.5 x 3.5 metres/11½ x 11½ feet, but they feel nicely proportioned, with the architectural structure of the chimney breasts creating useful alcoves on either side. The original cast-iron fireplaces are still in situ and provide each room with an elegant focal point, as well as a natural dictate as far as furniture positioning goes.

**THIS PAGE** Making the most of a tiny space requires careful consideration. A stripped-pine door adds character to a period house, but takes up valuable floor space when open. A neat, compact sofa in proportion with the rest of the furnishings is the perfect solution.

"KEEPING TO A SIMPLE AND RESTRAINED PALETTE OF ARCHITECTURAL DETAILS IS KEY TO CREATING A HARMONIOUS AND CALM INTERIOR, WHEN SPACE IS LIMITED."

"FURNISHING YOUR HOME WITH JUST A FEW HIGHLY TREASURED ITEMS WILL MAKE IT FEEL LIKE A VERY SPECIAL PLACE, NO MATTER HOW TINY IT MIGHT BE."

**THIS PAGE** Far from being cold and austere, the all-white palette of this pretty living room is 'lifted' by touches of soft taupe and silver and accessorized with an intricate collection of delicate porcelain, ceramic and glass. In the summer it is light and bright, and in winter, with the open fire, comfortably warm.

If conservation regulations had allowed, removing the original, central staircase could have created an open living/dining area, and more of a sense of space, but the repositioning of the stairs to the side of the house would have swallowed up a significant proportion of the smaller bedroom, leaving it with very little practical purpose at all. Another option might have been to remove the chimney breasts throughout, but that would have been a structural and costly exercise and, while gaining a little extra floor space, the rooms would have lost the alcoves, which are ideal for shelving, not to mention the valuable aesthetic potential of the fireplaces.

Despite its original humble status, the house delivers enormously on architectural detail, and as I am a firm believer of working with what you have rather than against it, it seemed only right that the modest and simple style of the house should be taken into consideration when making improvements. The windows, which are in perfect proportion to the rooms – each aperture is large enough to let in a lovely amount of light, but small enough to offer an element of privacy – have all been fitted throughout with wooden shutters in a classic, understated Shaker style that marries form and function

ABOVE Even in compact homes, period elements work well as the main focus of decoration. The original fireplace – once the only source of heating – makes a beautiful feature in this small room, and is complemented by industrial-style radiators and simple wood-panelled shutters that are in keeping with the utilitarian aesthetic.

FAR LEFT A porcelain wall-hanging that fringes the corner of the chimney breast and an unframed photograph propped up among the ceramic items create a feeling of calm in the living space.

LEFT A handmade china vase is the ideal container for a sprig of fresh flowers.

**LEFT** Ideas for storage range from the practical to the beautiful. In this room, woven-rush suitcases fit neatly under the bed and are used to store clothes tidily out of sight when not being worn.

**RIGHT** A pretty planted window box gives a small interior an essential connection with nature and the outdoors.

**BELOW LEFT** Keeping decoration to a minimum is very effective in a small room. Just a handful of treasured pieces and some warm textiles create a tranquil atmosphere.

"DECORATING A SMALL SPACE WITH AN ALL-WHITE COLOUR SCHEME ENCOURAGES THE EYE TO BE LED TO THE WINDOW AND THE VIEW OUTSIDE, THEREBY GIVING THE ILLUSION THAT IT IS MUCH LARGER IN SIZE THAN IT ACTUALLY IS."

so effortlessly. There is also a hugely practical element too, as they neatly fold back, allowing the maximum amount of light to enter the small rooms.

The backdrop of the interior is wholesome, with clean whitewashed walls and natural materials. The floorboards have been stripped, sanded and left bare so that the beauty of the wood can be enjoyed, while the upstairs ones were painted white for a subtle variation in pace. The wooden fire surrounds, also identical throughout, are modest in style but well carpentered and comfortably proportioned, and cupboards and a bumpy wall at the top of the stairs have been clad in practical and pleasingly regular tongue-and-groove panelling. All the walls and woodwork have been painted a unifying shade of white, and the inset shelves in all the rooms, bar the main bedroom, match with their clean lines and straightforward design, which is in keeping with the overall simple aesthetic. It is a short but prescriptive list

"EVERY OBJECT SHOULD HAVE A NATURAL HOME, AND IF IT DOES, IT MAKES THE TASK OF KEEPING A SMALL SPACE TIDY VERY STRAIGHTFORWARD INDEED."

**THIS PAGE** Sparely designed furniture pieces are invaluable in a small space. This utilitarian storage unit is roomy and has similar dimensions to a three-drawer alternative, but its configuration of nine compact sections creates a chic, slimline aesthetic. The choice of colour, a 'quiet' vanilla white, blends well with the rest of the décor.

of ingredients that has come together to create a design template that cleverly and subliminally connects the individual rooms, giving the illusion of greater space, while still affording them their own identity through the furnishings naturally dictated by their individual functions.

This also extends to some of the key decorative elements too, with delicate little porcelain collages above each of the fireplaces, classic bone china 'Hector' task lamps throughout and matching pendant lights in both of the bedrooms and also in both the downstairs rooms.

**THIS PAGE** Dual-purpose rooms are ideal in small spaces. A compact guest bedroom can easily double as a home office, for example. Here, a 1.2-metre/4-foot-wide antique bedstead is a good compromise between a single- and a double-sized modern alternative. It allows room for a work desk and has more space beneath, so plenty of storage potential too.

Despite its pared-back, elemental style, this is an exceptionally comfortable home, with luxurious details such as natural linens and warm wools in neutral shades interspersed with some fresh pastels and a vast array of lovely bits and pieces. It is an aesthetic where plain and simple neatly converge with nicely decorative, and, as the home of a stylist (still slightly biased!) who is well versed at editing and with a keen eye for detail, it goes without saying that it is very much a curated space. An attic – as yet unchartered potential renovation territory – provides plenty of out-of-sight storage for an archive of props and other things collected along the way, allowing the small living spaces to be afforded the luxury of less. Objects of all sorts are used to great effect to create displays of things that are both beautiful as well as useful. In the living room, random everyday items are placed alongside sculptural and delicately fragile pieces of biscuit porcelain that provide a touch of decorative embellishment, whereas in the dining room the displays consist of china, pretty glassware and pleasingly shaped practical objects such as wooden spoons and chopping boards that are an overspill from the tiny kitchen and just too lovely to be stored away in a drawer.

**ABOVE LEFT** Custom-built shelves set into an alcove turn an otherwise redundant corner into a compact home office with plenty of room for work files and books.

**ABOVE RIGHT** The bathroom is the smallest space in this period home. It occupies the area over the stairwell combined with a slice taken out of a previously larger second bedroom. The room is pretty and practical, and its design is in keeping with the rest of the interior. The styling is fresh and white, while a well-proportioned period-style basin and decorative mirror add feminine touches.

**OPPOSITE** Despite the apartment's tiny proportions and the limited budget that had been assigned to the project, Marianne chose a large marble breakfast bar to serve as a kitchen work surface as well as a place for Pauline to entertain friends. The quality of the material introduces a touch of luxury.

**FAR LEFT** Quirky lighting can make a great style statement in a small space. The angular design of this pendant shade nicely echoes the zigzag shape of the staircase.

**LEFT** A linen-covered mattress and some scatter cushions transform an empty corner into a comfortable spot for relaxation.

# COLOURFULLY COMPACT

THIS PRETTY PARISIAN PIED A TERRE IS A TRUE TESTAMENT TO THE IDEA THAT A LITTLE CREATIVITY CAN SOMETIMES GO AN AWFULLY LONG WAY. DUE TO ITS LIMITED SIZE – A MERE 25 SQUARE METRES/269 SQUARE FEET – AND AN EQUALLY LIMITED BUDGET, THE DILEMMA FOR OWNER PAULINE WAS HOW TO TRANSFORM THE FAMILY STUDIO IN CENTRAL PARIS INTO A SPACE FOR LIVING AND STUDYING FOR HERSELF AND HER PARTNER.

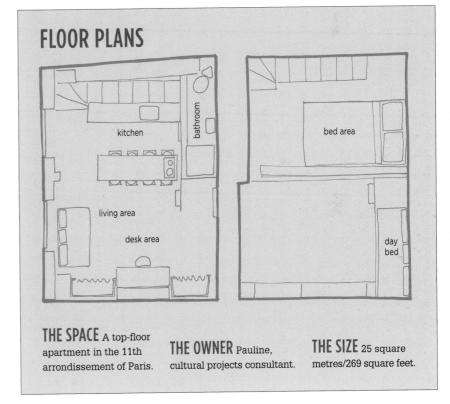

**FLOOR PLANS**

kitchen

bathroom

bed area

living area

desk area

day bed

**THE SPACE** A top-floor apartment in the 11th arrondissement of Paris.

**THE OWNER** Pauline, cultural projects consultant.

**THE SIZE** 25 square metres/269 square feet.

Purchased back in the late 1970s by Pauline's father, the flat has remained – as is so common in France – in the family ever since, becoming home to various friends and relatives along the way, but without ever being subject to any much-needed decorative improvement. While Pauline's enthusiasm for the potential transformation was key to its final success, the project needed expert help. She enlisted Marianne Evennou  a family friend and interior architect with

**THIS PICTURE** The staircase that leads up to the mezzanine appears to climb over the top of the kitchen and cleverly 'contains' it in its own section of the open-plan space.

with a great deal of experience in remodelling shoebox-sized Parisian interiors, to redesign the space and create a refreshed interior.

Marianne's philosophy for small-space interiors is very much about recognizing the need for different, clearly defined zones, so that even in a tiny apartment there is still a sense of moving from one area to another. Ideally, she prefers to create partitions with openings as a compromise between dividing walls and a completely open-plan layout, in order to keep the visual field as open as possible yet still offer some privacy. However, if an interior is too small to allow for this, Marianne is quick to impress that different areas for sleeping, cooking, eating, relaxing and working can be demarcated successfully by using different colours or patterns on the walls and floor. Marianne is also a firm believer in the importance of a hallway – no matter how small – to separate the internal space from that of the exterior. In Pauline's apartment, this works beautifully, as the hallway is hidden from the main living space by the wall connecting to the kitchen and is small enough not to take up too much valuable floor space, but large enough to provide Pauline with space for hanging coats and storing boots and shoes. It also, crucially, provides a psychological barrier between the inside of the apartment and the communal corridor outside.

The existing layout was very short on space, and the only option, despite the limited budget, was to access the roof space. What was previously a tangle of beams turned out to be the perfect place on which to build a mezzanine level that stretches from one end to the next. It creates not only a bed area for Pauline but also a separate lounging area and occasional guest bed too, as well as giving the apartment a great deal of architectural interest. The 'bedroom' has been made accessible by a clever staircase that appears to climb above the kitchen work surface and provides an alcove for the

MARIANNE: "IN A SMALL FLAT, IT IS ALL THE MORE NECESSARY TO HAVE MARKED-OUT AREAS FOR DIFFERENT FUNCTIONS AND TO BE VERY ORGANIZED IN ORDER TO LIVE HARMONIOUSLY.

compact kitchen to sit in. It is also another of the ingenious design features that give this tiny space its bold charm and character.

Marianne then prioritized the spending of the remainder of the budget for customizing the space to suit Pauline's love of cooking and entertaining, creating a luxuriously long marble breakfast bar. This also serves as a surface to hide valuable kitchen storage underneath, and acts as a low-level but interconnecting barrier between the living and cooking spaces. A tiny but fully functional shower room is tucked neatly behind a sliding door. While diminutive in size, it hasn't been overlooked when it comes to decorative details, with beautiful patterned floor tiles and a graphic ticking stripe curtain to hide the plumbing being sufficient embellishment to enliven such a small space.

The main floor, however, is perhaps the most striking decorative feature of the space and is the handiwork of Pauline, who painstakingly taped off and painted the different sections to create the effect of encaustic tiles, but at a fraction of the cost. Its graphic geometric pattern and the solid colours – deliberately slightly knocked back in tone to complement the shades on the walls – make a strong visual statement and set the mood for the rest of the furnishings and accessories. These range from the bright, square motifs on the sofa and floor cushion to the boldly

**OPPOSITE** The mainly monochrome tones of Pauline's office space are in complete contrast to the intense colours in the living space, giving each area its own clear identity. A simple fabric curtain hung from a metal pole is a cost-effective way to create a screen for hiding clutter.

**ABOVE LEFT** Tiny homes benefit from tiny accessories. A few stems of foliage in this unusual wall-mounted vase add a delicate touch to Pauline's work space.

**ABOVE CENTRE** Black and white patterns are clean and contemporary and make a bold statement in one corner of a room.

**ABOVE RIGHT** Made-to-measure shelving, with various height configurations to accommodate everything from tiny books to large files, is a great space saver.

striped curtains that act as cupboard doors and the tessellated black and white storage boxes. Even the work area, while not huge, displays a satisfying balance of graphic lines and orderly decorative detail provided by the custom-built shelving, the vintage-style door fronts designed to look like a set of filing drawers and a calm colour scheme.

Setting the architectural remodelling of the original space aside, this tiny home is very much a visual exposition on how clever interior design and a wonderful lively and structured mix of pattern, texture and bold colour can inject a small space with an unquestionably large sense of style and sophistication, and on a limited budget too.

**RIGHT** The vertical stripes of the curtain screening Pauline's storage cupboard lead the eye up to the mezzanine level, used for relaxation, which is one of her favourite parts of the studio. The vintage wooden ladder came from a local flea market.

**FAR RIGHT** A space-saving, industrial-style sliding door leads into the bathroom. A handful of patterned tiles and the restrained palette of black, white and grey give this tiny room a highly contemporary feel.

**BELOW RIGHT** What was once redundant loft space has been used by the architect to create a roomy mezzanine above the hallway with sleeping platforms at both ends. A variety of striped textiles chosen by Pauline has been scattered throughout the apartment to enhance its decorative cohesion.

PAULINE: "ONE OF MY FAVOURITE SPOTS IS THE DAYBED ON THE MEZZANINE. IT IS LIKE BEING PERCHED UP IN A TREE HOUSE."

"THE ARCHITECTURAL AND BUDGET RESTRAINTS HAD BENEFICIAL EFFECTS, AS THEY WERE A GREAT SOURCE OF INSPIRATION."

**THIS PAGE** The exposed structural wooden beams are superb architectural features that form ready-made partitions between the two mezzanine spaces. Tiny alcoves in the far corner, positioned next to the staircase down to the kitchen, provide useful storage space.

**RIGHT** Grasses from the beach displayed in a large jar give the interior a link with its surroundings. The glass jars are beautifully transparent and airy in feel.

**FAR RIGHT** Vintage metal 'Tolix' chairs used by the family during meals can be stacked neatly in a corner when not needed.

**OPPOSITE** Making use of the roof space, the owners have created a stunning mezzanine level, accessed by a nautically inspired ladder. It adds architectural interest to this small weekend retreat, as well as functional sleeping space.

# NEAT AND NAUTICAL

SET JUST A STONE'S THROW FROM THE BEACH ON THE RUGGED COASTLINE OF DENMARK'S ISLAND OF FUNEN, ONE OF THE MANY THAT MAKE UP THIS SCATTERED ARCHIPELAGO, THIS DELIGHTFUL SUMMERHOUSE BEAUTIFULLY EPITOMIZES THE CHARM THAT SMALL-SPACE LIVING CAN OFFER. WHILE IT CLEARLY SERVES AS MATERIAL FOR WISTFUL DAYDREAMING, IT ALSO OFFERS AN ENORMOUS AMOUNT OF INSPIRATION FOR DESIGNING AND DECORATING A TINY INTERIOR.

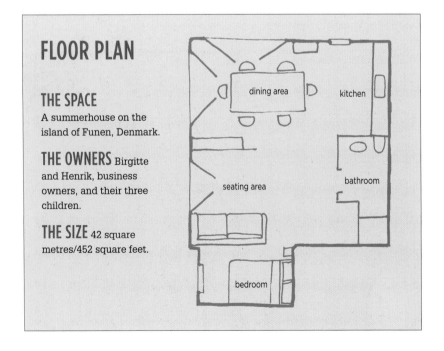

## FLOOR PLAN

### THE SPACE
A summerhouse on the island of Funen, Denmark.

### THE OWNERS
Birgitte and Henrik, business owners, and their three children.

### THE SIZE
42 square metres/452 square feet.

dining area

kitchen

bathroom

seating area

bedroom

Dating back to the 1920s, the summerhouse is one of several along the coast that, come the warmer months and the almost endless hours of daylight, transform this quiet coastal spot into a thriving and lively seaside retreat. Life is very much about spending time out of doors, and the house, with its large wraparound wooden deck, has been carefully planned to allow its owners to completely enjoy the natural seascape that lies outside.

Birgitte and Henrik run a business just 15 kilometres/9½ miles away in the nearby town of Kerteminde, and the quiet rural setting of the summerhouse provides a welcome contrast to their town life. The landscape here is still

"THE MEZZANINE LEVEL IS LOVED JUST AS MUCH BY ADULTS AS CHILDREN, AND IS GREAT FOR STORAGE TOO."

**ABOVE** The dining area is where the family often gathers. In the summer the doors are opened, connecting the inside with an exterior decked area. In winter, the log-burning stove and the sheepskin throws provide ample heat and warmth.

**OPPOSITE** The cathedral-like ceiling is a wonderful interior feature that gives this compact home a great sense of light and space. The soft blue of the walls changes from a fresh glassy shade of aquamarine during the day to a warm pebble grey as the light fades.

very much as it has been for the past 250 years, with lots of castles, historic buildings and orchards.

The house is used all year round, so it has to deliver on practicality and comfort for all seasons. Compact but with high ceilings, it feels luxuriously spacious yet nicely intimate as well, due to its clever layout and design. The functional areas of the house – the kitchen and bathroom – are tucked away along the rear wall of the house and are the only parts that aren't afforded stunning beach views.

Above here, a mezzanine sleeping area accessed by a slim, unobtrusive ladder makes use of the elevated roof space and enjoys views out to sea. Below is the bathroom, with the kitchen positioned on one side and a snug reading nook on the other, mirroring the linear layout of the kitchen and offering the eye some architectural symmetry and balance.

The rest of the space, bar the main bedroom at the far end of the house, is a living and socializing one that enjoys close proximity to the numerous sets of double doors leading outside. This is a

"DESPITE BEING A SMALL HOUSE, IT FEELS SO MUCH BIGGER BECAUSE OF THE GENEROUS CEILING HEIGHT."

"THE INTERIOR IS TRANSFORMED WITH ALL THE DOORS AND WINDOWS. IT'S FANTASTIC TO BE HERE IN THE SUMMER BECAUSE EVEN WHEN YOU ARE INSIDE IT FEELS LIKE BEING OUTSIDE. AND EVEN WHEN YOU ARE INSIDE DURING WINTER STORMS YOU REALLY FEEL YOU ARE IN THE MIDDLE OF NATURE."

house that is inextricably linked to its location. In summertime, the doors stand open onto the deck, with the pebble beach and sea just beyond. In winter, when the amount of daylight is significantly reduced, the emphasis is on the cosy corners inside the house, dressed with woollen textiles, Scandinavian sheepskins, candles and lanterns that all combine to create a cosy – or, as the Danish would say, 'hygge' – atmosphere. This part of Denmark is very dark at night, so the stars appear to shine particularly brightly. For the owners, there is no better way to feel protected from the elements than when cocooned in the house looking up to the vast expanse of black, diamond-studded sky through the skylights in the roof.

Practical winter warmers are also on hand in the shape of a large log burner and wooden cladding on the walls that in summer provides the perfect nautical aesthetic but in winter offers insulation and textural warmth. The main bedroom is perfectly shipshape, being just the right length for a double bed and creating a charming cabin-style sleeping space with an uninterrupted view out to sea. Round mirrors act as 'portholes', consistent with the maritime-inspired décor elsewhere, and a slim custom-built wardrobe neatly slots into the room to make the most of what is a very tiny space.

There are so many inspiring ideas for small interiors that work wonderfully here, cleverly maximizing the sense of space yet retaining an element of restfulness in the interior.

**OPPOSITE** A pretty rattan chair and lightweight vintage stool have been placed by the French doors that open onto the beach, making a light-filled corner for relaxing and enjoying the summer breeze.

**ABOVE RIGHT** A cosy reading nook built into an alcove incorporates some useful shelving. Underneath are drawers on castors that can be pulled out for ease of use.

**RIGHT** A contemporary two-seater sofa – streamlined in design and compact in size – is the ideal seating solution for any small interior. The footstool in coordinating fabric doubles as a side table.

**RIGHT** The bedroom is nautical in both style and function, with a small double bed that fits snugly inside in a fashion reminiscent of a ship's cabin. The sliding door, porthole mirrors and blue and grey tones are all in keeping with the maritime aesthetic.

**BELOW** The half-height partition between the living and dining areas makes a handy shelf for the display of pebbles and shells.

The wood cladding is painted a soft blue shade that changes in tone as often as the watery seascape out of the window, depending on the amount of natural light. The living area is cleverly divided with a simple low-level partition that is just high enough to provide a sense of separation between the living and dining spaces, but also just low enough not to be an awkward or restrictive barrier. Sliding pocket doors on both the bedroom and bathroom are great space savers, and various creative storage solutions have been introduced to keep the family's clutter tucked away. The little reading nook has useful drawers on castors beneath, complemented visually by a set of rattan boxes on the shelves above, and in the kitchen a slimline plate rack, reminiscent of those in a ship's galley, provides a stylish way to store tableware. Although its clever design with front lips to stop the plates from moving around while at sea isn't necessary here, it is nevertheless yet another nicely nautical touch.

**THIS PAGE** It is essential in a tiny bathroom to create visual interest. Here, an elegant carved wooden table has been painted and modified to accommodate the plumbing for a counter-top basin. The pretty mirror is a complementary feature.

**RIGHT** Lightweight furniture, such as this classic mid-century rocker by Charles and Ray Eames, is a boon in small spaces. In addition, this chair's vivid shade of peacock blue packs a visual punch.

**FAR RIGHT** An adjustable narrow shelving unit tucked into an alcove offers useful display and storage space.

**OPPOSITE** The transformation of this small apartment has been achieved by installing a glass-panelled partition between the sleeping area and the rest of the open-plan interior, and by using a fashionably dark and intense colour palette.

# SHADES OF GREY
THIS APARTMENT IN THE FRENCH CITY OF LYON IS A FABULOUS EXAMPLE OF HOW DARK SHADES CAN BE USED TO DRAMATIC EFFECT IN A TINY SPACE. DESPITE MEASURING JUST 35 SQUARE METRES/377 SQUARE FEET — THE SAME DIMENSIONS AS ITS ALL-WHITE COUNTERPART SITUATED ON THE FLOOR ABOVE (SEE PAGES 78–85), BUT STYLED VERY DIFFERENTLY — THIS CHIC APARTMENT CONTAINS ALL THE ELEMENTS A MODERN LIVING SPACE DEMANDS.

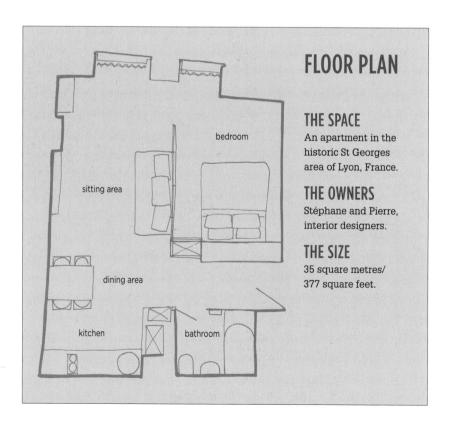

## FLOOR PLAN

### THE SPACE
An apartment in the historic St Georges area of Lyon, France.

### THE OWNERS
Stéphane and Pierre, interior designers.

### THE SIZE
35 square metres/ 377 square feet.

Situated in a charming 16th-century stone building nestled among the meandering cobbled streets of the St Georges district — a UNESCO-accredited World Heritage site and part of the historic quarter of Vieux Lyon — this is one of two apartments in the same building that are the creative work of interior design duo Stéphane and Pierre. Despite being bought and designed specifically to be used as medium-to short-term lets, offering visitors to the city a comfortable and stylish rental experience, the two apartments contain a wealth of style ideas and practical design solutions that can be used as a source of inspiration for interiors that are intended as a permanent residence.

"IT IS IMPORTANT TO
EVALUATE THE SPACE WELL
TO GIVE THE IMPRESSION
THAT NOTHING IS MISSING
IN TERMS OF COMFORT."

With space in very short supply, the designers chose to keep the apartment as open plan as possible. After factoring in enough room for a good-sized bathroom with a full-sized tub, what would otherwise be a bland studio apartment has been redesigned to create a compact and chic one-bedroomed space, thanks to the addition of a simple but effective floor-to-ceiling, partly glazed L-shaped wall. This effectively partitions off a corner of the space to accommodate a double bed and offer some privacy, but still provides ample space in the main area for relaxing.

The Crittall-style glass-panelled wall, with its smart and contemporary industrial-style aesthetic, acts as a striking architectural focal point and contributes significantly to the elegance and atmosphere of the apartment. However, it is a very practical element too, thanks to the clever combination of glass panels and a solid bottom section, and the proportions of each. The glass panels allow natural light from the two windows to reach to the back of the apartment and also draw the eye through the glass to the outside, creating an impression

**OPPOSITE** Attention to detail is key to creating a sense of balance in the design of small interiors. In this room, the impact of bold statement pieces such as the industrial-style radiator and the retro wood cupboard is softened by their juxtaposition with the comfortable couch, the textural linen cushions and the woollen rug.

**ABOVE** Cleverly incorporated in the shelving system, and surrounded by an intriguing mix of curios and framed pictures, the television does not distract from the overall aesthetic.

**LEFT** The dark frame of the glass partition is in bold contrast to the soft grey of the walls. It acts as a design feature in its own right, picking up and reflecting other elements of the space such as the vertical straight line of the floor light and the graphic square shapes of the cupboard doors.

**ABOVE LEFT** In a confined area, a curtain is a space-saving alternative to cupboard doors. Here, however, the effect is more about style than function. The addition of the curtain allows the kitchen to be less defined by its purpose within the open-plan interior.

**ABOVE RIGHT** Teaming warm woods with dark metallics gives the apartment a modern rustic vibe, which is also evident in the choice of kitchen accessories.

**RIGHT** A large wall-mounted light with a pure white shade is both bright and bold, and provides the small dining space with a sense of drama and occasion.

of openness and space. At the same time, a sense of separation is maintained between the two spaces, as the bed is concealed by the solid bottom section of the wall, which is just tall enough to hide it while allowing for as much glass as possible. An essential storage space for clothes has been neatly tucked into the hallway, enabling the small bedroom area to be a luxurious and uncluttered corner of the apartment.

But the defining element of the design of the interior has to be its décor. Stéphane and Pierre opted for a fashionable palette of soft mid-grey for the walls, teamed with intense shades of rich black and inky blue, and they have kept as much of the decoration as possible within the same tonal range of these colours. The result is an interior that is interesting without being complicated, and also one that is intimate and snug but feels much bigger than it appears on plan, due to the couple's clever design tricks.

"THE INDIVIDUAL ELEMENTS IN A SMALL SPACE ARE IMPORTANT, BUT WHAT IS MOST IMPORTANT IS HOW YOU MIX THEM TOGETHER AND THE DIFFERING SCALE AND PROPORTIONS BETWEEN THEM."

**BELOW** Creative solutions for small spaces are often the most stylish. A wall-mounted industrial task light and slimline shelf are interesting options for a bedside table.

The lateral configuration of the planks of roughly hewn wood cladding that cover the main wall is deliberate and not only serves to guide the eye down the length of the apartment, giving the illusion of a larger space, but also acts as a counterpoint to the vertical lines of the glazed partition wall, providing a subliminal connection between the two spaces while allowing each to retain its own individuality.

In a similar vein, different areas of the interior are segregated by clever use of accessories. Two large, graphic patterned floor rugs clearly define the dining and living areas, but their similarities in colour and style serve to provide a cohesive link between the areas within the space as a whole.

It is the inclusion of ideas such as these that elevate this tiny space's potential and enable it to deliver on style and sophistication  The dark, moody palette is softened by an abundance of downlighters — task lamps, table lamps and pendants — which create individual pools of light that enhance the cosy atmosphere. A chic, low-level caravanserai-style sofa provides luxuriant lounging, while furniture in reclaimed wood and textures in soft slubby linens and natural wools add softness. Along with a quirky mix of vintage ethnic, modern rustic and contemporary statement pieces, all combine to create an interior that, though small in size, is most certainly big on personality.

**THIS PAGE** The partition wall made of glass and wood successfully separates the sleeping area from the rest of the interior yet still allows a sense of connectivity. Textiles used in the linen headboard and duvet and pillow covers are in the same shades of inky blue as seen in the living space.

"WHEN DESIGNING AN INTERIOR, PARTICULARLY IF IT IS SMALL, IT IS IMPORTANT TO CONSIDER WHO WILL LIVE IN IT AND THEIR WAY OF LIFE."

**OPPOSITE** Pierre and Stéphane have transformed the space into an elegant interior and one that feels much larger than it is. The voluminous rattan pendant lamp and assortment of chairs create a play on scale and proportion that leads to an illusion of spaciousness.

**FAR LEFT** Classic picture panelling that has been painted the same colour as the rest of the interior subtly demarcates the area reserved for dining.

**LEFT** Storage solutions don't have to be complicated. For example, a capacious Kilner jar makes a sweet alternative to a cutlery/flatware tray.

# A TRAVELLER'S TALE AS KEEN TRAVELLERS, DESIGNERS STEPHANE AND PIERRE OF MAISON HAND RETURN FROM BUYING TRIPS ABROAD WITH HEADS FULL OF VISUAL INSPIRATION AS WELL AS SUITCASES FULL OF PURCHASES. TRAVELLING AROUND THE WORLD AND STAYING IN ALL SORTS OF HOTEL ROOMS ALONG THE WAY, THE COUPLE HAVE DISCOVERED SOME INSPIRING IDEAS FOR BALANCING HARMONIOUS LIVING WITH PRACTICALITY IN SMALL SPACES.

The calm, serene and sophisticated ethnic décor of this light, bright apartment is very much a style anthology of the best features of some of those hotel rooms. It is also a fusion of the couple's original design intentions, which hark back to their first business in home decoration – an interiors boutique called Hand, also based in Lyon – that specialized in combining handmade one-off items with a charming global mix sourced from all over.

When the pair set themselves a design brief for this apartment, they drew on their elegant yet ethnic aesthetic and a sense of being abroad. They also wanted to achieve a feeling of relaxation and wellbeing, despite the

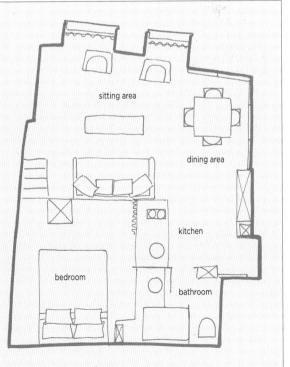

## FLOOR PLAN

### THE SPACE
An apartment in the historic St Georges area of Lyon, France.

### THE OWNERS
Stéphane and Pierre, interior designers.

### THE SIZE
35 square metres/ 377 square feet.

sitting area

dining area

kitchen

bedroom

bathroom

**THIS PAGE** Compact and contained indeed: although this kitchen is very small, it includes all the essentials for preparing and cooking food. A simple hanging rail is the perfect solution for storing utensils, as well as making a lovely display feature.

**RIGHT** Mixing old and new is a great way of adding visual interest in a small space. A vintage wooden cupboard has been given a new lease of life with a coat of white paint and provides valuable extra storage for kitchen china and glassware.

**BELOW RIGHT** A compact shower room is ideal in a tiny apartment. Pierre and Stéphane have decorated it in the same utilitarian style as the nearby kitchen. Basic white tiles and black grouting make a bold style statement.

## "WE TRAVEL A LOT AND WE ALWAYS TRY TO TAKE INSPIRATION FROM WHAT WE SEE. HOTEL SUITES ARE GREAT FOR SMALL-SPACE IDEAS."

apartment's restrictions in size. So two armchairs were brought back from China, the baskets on the wall from a trip to Burma, the oversized lamps are from Indonesia and the carpet from Morocco.

There are many influences present in this small space, yet they work wonderfully well together, thanks to the similar textures provided by the natural wood and the rustic bamboo and rattan, offset by the calming soft white shade chosen for the walls. It's a tried-and-tested palette of colours and materials that Stéphane and Pierre have applied to several of Maison Hand's interior decorating projects, and which works particularly well in such a small space. The subtle greyish-green off-white paint used on the walls offers an ethereal sense of space, but also a feeling of warmth as it is nicely 'lifted' and thrown into contrast by the pure white-painted floor. The sense of spaciousness also owes much to the large mirror

placed in the corner at floor level, which provides a highly effective and much-needed visual expansion of the living space, and the accompanying mirrored cubes with low-level table lamps. More elaborate details include the decorative gilt mirrors above the bed and the woven wicker baskets on the wall of the living area. Both are perfect examples of how to create a display in a small interior by grouping a few similar objects together to provide visual interest but without fuss or clutter.

Yet this small space has more to offer than what is on the walls. A compact shower room and small fitted kitchen allow for more space to be allocated to the key design component of this studio space: the raised bedroom area with built-in closet. This is screened off by large partition windows that provide privacy at night time and connectivity to the rest of the space during the day. Just three steps separate the two levels, but

THIS PAGE Interesting decorative pieces sourced by the couple during their travels abroad give the small apartment a touch of global grandeur. Mixing quirky, one-off finds with functional pieces adds personality and style to any compact space.

they divide the apartment into a clearly defined living area and a sleeping space to retreat to in the evening. The raised bedroom also cleverly accommodates a built-in closet that occupies the area above the kitchen cupboards, thereby utilizing what would otherwise be redundant space. Likewise, the washing machine is tucked beneath the sleeping area and accessed by a little door.

The pair have used some classic small-space solutions to great effect and, by combining these with their own inimitable style, have created an intimate yet attractive and sophisticated space. A vintage cupboard has been given a rough coat of paint and offers a wonderful visual contrast to the clean uniformity of the fitted kitchen cabinets, and provides additional space for crockery, cutlery/flatware

**THIS PAGE** A pretty display of similar but slightly different rattan baskets on the wall offers plenty of visual interest without being overly complicated. Mirrors generate reflections and make the most of the available daylight, enhancing the overall sense of space; and a calming mix of soft textures and breezy shades creates a living area that is relaxed and welcoming.

and other kitchen essentials. In the dining area, the panelling on the wall, painted the same shade, quietly but convincingly defines the dining area from the rest of the open-plan living space, with the individual panels acting like empty picture frames and providing additional visual interest without the need for a great deal of artwork. The oversized ceiling lamps and imposing wooden Chinese armchairs are a play on scale and proportion when teamed with other pieces in the apartment of a more regular size.

Similar tiling has been used to marry together two tiny spaces – the shower room and the kitchen – that sit closely together. And repetition abounds, but subliminally so: the graphic framing of the black grout on the white tiles has been picked up and echoed in other details such as the pattern on the rug, the pictures on the walls and the black trim on the shades of the floor lamps and even on the curtains and hooks and poles in the closet. Subtle and simple ideas these may be, but they are also surprisingly effective.

"WE LIKE TO MIX DIFFERENT STYLES, SO THERE ARE MODERN PIECES OF FURNITURE FROM OUR SHOP BUT ALSO VINTAGE PIECES THAT WE BOUGHT AT THE FLEA MARKET, ALL ADDING LOTS OF INTEREST."

**RIGHT** The raised sleeping area is what makes this small space work so well. Only a few steps separate it from the rest of the apartment but they make it feel like a separate room. Glass panels have been installed above the level of the bed to screen it out of sight during the daytime and curtains can be drawn to block out the light at night.

**BELOW LEFT** Utilizing any redundant space is key to making the most of compact interiors. Part of the area underneath the sleeping platform has been used to house the washing machine rather than trying to squeeze it into the tiny kitchen.

**BELOW RIGHT** An empty alcove in the bedroom area makes the perfect cubbyhole for clothes storage. A hanging rail and linen curtain transform the empty corner into a stylish alternative to a wardrobe. The false glass aperture between the bedroom and bathroom admits as much light as possible into the otherwise windowless space.

**RIGHT** Despite its smallness, the bedroom oozes style. The generous-sized bed is layered with soft and luxurious linens and blankets in neutral tones. Two wall-mounted bedside lamps and a tidy arrangement of pillows create symmetry, while a random display of ornate wall mirrors provides a contrasting informality and a decadent and extravagant feast for the eye.

**RIGHT** Contemporary pops of colour enliven the predominately white interior. A kitchen wall has been painted a fresh aqua and acts as a chalk board for the couple's son Adrian.

**FAR RIGHT** Kristina's surplus painting supplies are kept in storage boxes that double as seating in the living space.

**OPPOSITE** The small open-plan kitchen/dining/working area is light, bright and white. The rubber flooring was in place when the couple moved in but harmonizes with the slimline furniture and Arash's own-design pendant light to increase the sense of space.

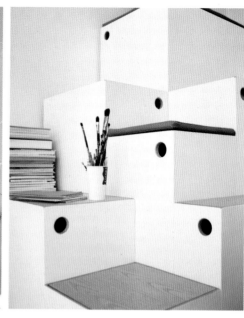

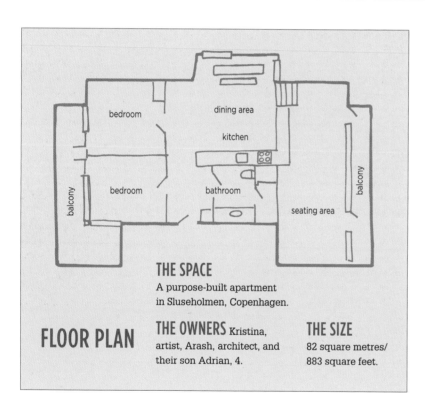

## FLOOR PLAN

**THE SPACE**
A purpose-built apartment in Sluseholmen, Copenhagen.

**THE OWNERS** Kristina, artist, Arash, architect, and their son Adrian, 4.

**THE SIZE**
82 square metres/ 883 square feet.

# LITTLE BOXES

A DOUBLE DILEMMA FOR KRISTINA AND ARASH LED TO SOME SERIOUSLY CREATIVE THINKING AND A SERIOUSLY COOL SOLUTION. THEIR SMALL APARTMENT, ON THE PENINSULA OF SLUSEHOLMEN, IN THE SOUTH HARBOUR AREA OF COPENHAGEN, NEEDED TO FUNCTION BOTH AS A FAMILY HOME AND A WORK SPACE. IT IS ALSO A RENTAL PROPERTY, SO THE EXTENT TO WHICH THEY COULD RECONFIGURE THE SPACE TO SATISFY THEIR GROWING NEEDS WAS LIMITED.

Located in a modern apartment block, one of several specifically designed to cater for Copenhagen's growing number of families, single people and retirees, this apartment is in an area that's much sought after, due to its vibrant mix of people and its strong sense of community living. Once home to some of the city's heavy industry, Sluseholmen is now regenerated, primarily residential and exceptionally tranquil and quiet, with stunning views over the harbour. Kristina and Arash's apartment enjoys a picturesque location overlooking a row of brightly painted wooden huts,

"ANOTHER DETAIL THAT WORKS IS THE SEATING ARRANGEMENT AROUND THE DINING/OFFICE TABLE. USING BENCHES MAKES THE ARRANGEMENT LOOK LIGHTER THAN HAVING SIX OR EIGHT CHAIRS OR STOOLS INSTEAD."

belonging to the former boat club, which add a sense of character to the area as well as creating a lovely juxtaposition of old and new.

Despite being small in size, the layout of this ground-floor apartment is well considered, and affords its inhabitants two compact bedrooms and a small but adequate bathroom. A simple design aesthetic ensures they are clean and uncluttered – Kristina and Arash's bedroom consists of just a bed, and all clothes storage is accommodated in a bank of units in their son Adrian's bedroom, concealed behind a curtain. This means the majority of the interior is devoted to an open-plan arrangement with a kitchen/dining area looking out onto, and leading down to, the small but light and bright living room, with its high ceilings and large east-facing windows. The shell of the interior has been kept pure white in keeping with Arash's liking for minimalist spaces, which works well with the volume of daylight that floods in, and also for Kristina's painting. But the couple also have a love of colour, and while adding it to walls is a quick and cost-effective way of personalizing a rental space, they opted instead to use it as a highlight. So they selected a palette of cool blues and greens for painting internal

OPPOSITE A simple internal door has been transformed by a coat of cheerful turquoise paint. Adding splashes of vibrant colour is a great way to create pockets of visual interest in a small interior.

LEFT A clean and simple modern design has been chosen for the compact kitchen. An assortment of drawer sizes and cupboard configurations offers a wealth of storage options, and inset appliances are great space-savers too.

BELOW Modern kitchens are often designed with space-saving solutions in mind, such as this pull-out storage drawer in what would otherwise be an unused area behind the plinth boards.

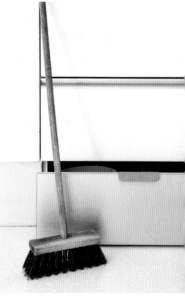

"I THINK THE BEST WAY TO LIVE IN A SMALL APARTMENT IS TO MAKE A LOT OF ANY POTENTIAL AREAS FOR INTEGRATED STORAGE SPACE. 'LESS IS MORE' ESPECIALLY APPLIES TO SMALL SPACES, SO THE MORE YOU CAN PUT AWAY OUT OF SIGHT THE BETTER."

**THIS PAGE** Arash and Kristina's ingenious box design combines storage with seating at various heights to make the most of the views from the top part of the windows. As unique and visually appealing as they are practical, the boxes contain everything from Kristina's canvases to shoes and toys.

doors and the 'library' stepladder, a chalk wall in the kitchen, and for textiles and soft furnishings.

With both Kristina and Arash working primarily from home, the apartment has to work hard. The dining table doubles as a desk for Arash, and the high walls in the living space are where Kristina positions her canvases to paint. But what the space clearly lacked, and what the couple so desperately needed, was storage space – and in container-load proportions – to hold all their work stuff, household items and Adrian's toys too. Being creative, they wanted to find a solution that would maximize the 'vacant' space created by the high ceiling in the living room yet retain the best of the view outside. The result, a combination of Arash's architectural experience and Kristina's artistic thinking, is the ingenious 'building block' storage and seating area built by Arash himself. Very much a prototype, it is an easily adaptable idea that can be reconfigured in all sorts of ways for all sorts of different small spaces and, as

"VISUALLY, I THINK IT HELPS IN A SMALL SPACE TO LIFT THINGS OFF THE FLOOR WHERE POSSIBLE AND USE THE WALLS, LIKE WE DID WITH THE BOOKSHELF. IT ENABLES THE EYE TO SEE THE ENTIRE FLOOR SPACE, MAKING THE ROOM FEEL BIGGER."

**ABOVE** The shelves are tightly packed with an extensive collection of books that forms a natural and colourful display feature. Kristina and Arash spray-painted a metal stepladder in turquoise as a quirky alternative to a library-style one.

**LEFT** The lower floor of the split-level living space is anchored by Kristina's super-sized canvases and the mountainous stacks of books against the wall.

it isn't built in, is highly portable, so perfect for renters. The storage-cum-seating unit consists of 17 boxes made of birch wood ply and painted white, with a push-up hole in each to enable removal of the ash lid and provide access to the storage space inside. The largest box is 2 metres/ 6½ feet high and was designed specifically to house Kristina's canvases. The others are packed with clothes, prototypes of Arash's design work, sculptures, Adrian's toys and anything and everything else.

The configuration of the different-sized boxes creates cosy and intimate seating and lounging areas, the mattress doubling up as a guest bed, while the step-like formation echoes the dynamic already created by the split-level structure of the apartment. Accentuated with just a handful of super-sized accessories – an enormous industrial station clock, a task lamp of gigantic proportions and monumental columns of books that climb the walls – the unit provides the room and its high ceilings with a sense of drama in what might otherwise have been a simple and undistinguished small space.

**ABOVE** While children's bedrooms are often the smaller rooms in a home, they can still be full of fun ideas. Kristina and Arash hand-drew the woodland mural and added hooks to the illustration so that bags and coats could be hung from the 'tree'.

**ABOVE RIGHT** Shelves filled with some of Adrian's favourite toys and books add a dash of welcome colour to the tiny room.

**OPPOSITE** The couple's small bedroom faces the communal courtyard, so Kristina invested in luxuriously long and full curtains. Instead of cramming furniture into the space, they opted for just a bed and put storage for clothes in a corner of Adrian's bedroom. The area under the bed was kept empty to maximize the sense of space.

**RIGHT** A display of ornate candlesticks and antique silverware offers a rich flavour and some elegant charm to an essentially minimalist interior.

**FAR RIGHT** To make good use of the space available, two spacious cupboards have been built into the area under the stairs.

**OPPOSITE** A linen tablecloth transforms a basic table and set of chairs into an elegant entertaining area. The furniture pieces are folded flat and stored in a cupboard when not in use.

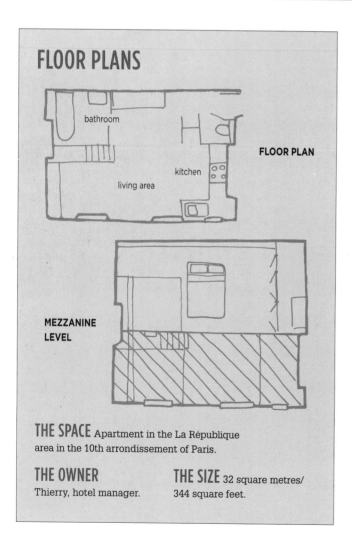

## FLOOR PLANS

bathroom

FLOOR PLAN

kitchen

living area

MEZZANINE LEVEL

**THE SPACE** Apartment in the La République area in the 10th arrondissement of Paris.

**THE OWNER**
Thierry, hotel manager.

**THE SIZE** 32 square metres/ 344 square feet.

# LIGHT AND BRIGHT FIRST IMPRESSIONS OF THIS TINY, TOP-FLOOR PARISIAN APARTMENT ARE, SURPRISINGLY, OF SPACIOUSNESS. AN ABUNDANCE OF NATURAL LIGHT FLOODS IN FROM THE SOUTHWEST THROUGH THE LARGE WINDOWS THAT RUN THE LENGTH OF THE OUTSIDE WALL, OPENING UP THE INTERIOR AND MAKING IT FEEL SIGNIFICANTLY MORE SIZEABLE THAN ITS COMPACT 32 SQUARE METRES/344 SQUARE FEET.

On further inspection, it is clear that the effect of space and light is not just thanks to the apartment's naturally sunny aspect but also to some clever architectural and interior design details that make full use of the roof space and accompanying high ceilings.

The apartment has been home to its owner, Thierry, for more than 20 years, and was originally purchased as a basic studio without the now much-valued additional roof space, and when the La République area was less gentrified than it is today. Despite having outgrown the original space, Thierry was reluctant to leave this vibrant, much sought-after and

**LEFT** Thierry's sectional sofa is a versatile seating choice. As a single, joined unit, the corner configuration creates a space for relaxing and acts as a partition between the entrance hall and the open-plan living space. The sofa also converts into a chaise longue and separate chair.

**RIGHT** To compensate for the lack of a separate dining area, Thierry has incorporated a small pedestal table and two high chairs into the kitchen corner. This small-space solution is streamlined and fuss free.

very central part of Paris, which lies close to the key stations Gare du Nord and Gare de l'Est, and minutes away from the newly redesigned and bustling Place de La République. The only option was a total remodelling of the interior.

Familiar with the space's positives and negatives, Thierry had his own ideas as to what was needed. Keen to have a separate bathroom, a fully equipped kitchen and as much cupboard space as possible, the only other specification he gave to architect Sylvie Cahen was to create a neat, simple aesthetic and a

practical interior that was easy to live in. As a hotel manager, Thierry is well versed in the benefits, practically and stylistically, of good storage, as well as all those other little design and build details that make small spaces really perform.

Working with Sylvie's ideas, the first step to maximizing the full potential of the place was to purchase the roof space, previously part of the communal area of the block of apartments and used for storage. This allowed Sylvie to strip back the entire space, removing all the partition walls and leaving just the bare

"MY APARTMENT IS LIKE MY IDEAL HOTEL ROOM, PLUS A KITCHEN CORNER. ALL I NEED IS AT HAND, EASILY REACHABLE, EASILY STORABLE."

**THIS PAGE** The built-in box elements were designed to be lower than the structural beams to give the impression that they are movable and that there is something behind them. This adds to the illusion of spaciousness.

"I HAVE TRIED TO AVOID FRAGMENTING THE SPACE AS MUCH AS POSSIBLE BECAUSE THE EMPTY SPACES ARE AS IMPORTANT AS THE CONTAINED ONES. THE STRATEGY WITH SUCH SMALL SPACES IS TO APPLY A HOLISTIC TREATMENT TO THE LAYOUT."

skeleton of the space. Capitalizing fully on the position of the windows and the rectangular shape of the structural frame, the empty shell was redesigned to contain two 'boxes': one for the kitchen, which sits on the light-filled side of the room; and one for the bathroom, which is tucked away from the windows, and below a mezzanine level that extends across the entire length of the space.

The mezzanine consists of two connecting platforms, with the lower section being home to a valuable work space, and the slightly higher one designated the sleeping area, with a bank of additional and much-used storage cleverly tucked in at the far end of the bedroom space.

The redesign certainly ticks all Thierry's requests for storage, with ample closet space concealed behind the run of cupboards in the main living space as well as the hallway. Even the space under the staircase is fully utilized, with additional storage space hidden underneath and accessed via simple doors for an exceptionally neat and clean aesthetic. All the constructed elements – the kitchen cabinets and the tall cupboards – don't extend right to the ceiling, but, like the 'boxes' that hold the bathroom and kitchen, have a floating space at the top, giving the impression that they are movable. This reinforces the impression that the apartment is larger and more capacious than it really is.

**LEFT** The bathroom is located in the box under the mezzanine level. It is hidden behind a sliding door, away from the main open-plan area. Since there is little natural daylight, Thierry has chosen a luxuriously dark and moody interior for a touch of boutique-hotel style at home.

**BELOW** Thierry's bed is on the mezzanine level, tucked under the sloping roof. The architect has incorporated additional low-level storage cupboards at the far end of the eaves.

The design objective was to create a small space that gives the feeling of being a far larger one, and to preserve as much of the unity of the space as possible. This meant paring back and keeping detail to a minimum, so the furnishings, materials and colours used throughout are limited but well considered. A modular sofa acts as a natural partition between the entrance and living space and is in keeping with the rest of the décor, while the low-level media/storage unit that sits in front of it is equally unobtrusive in style. Warm natural wood flooring seamlessly connects the spaces and the stairs, and a clever combination of white and light grey are used on the walls to great effect.

Despite Thierry's initial desire to decorate the entire apartment in bright, pure white, on Sylvie's recommendation it was finally restricted to the kitchen area and the two facing walls, and a serene shade of dove grey was used on all the custom-built constructed elements, such as the cupboards. It's a subtle off-white tone that, depending on the intensity of the light, displays numerous different variations in hue throughout the day – light in the morning, darkening with some cloud cover and resonating further in tone towards the evening – bringing an additional sense of atmosphere, warmth and mood to this nicely elegant and beautifully contained little space.

"WHEN A SMALL SPACE IS RATIONALLY ORGANIZED AND NICELY DESIGNED, IT CAN BE REALLY COMFORTABLE AND PLEASANT."

**THIS PAGE** Without the extra roof space, the original interior was cramped. What had once been the storage space for the entire block of apartments was purchased by Thierry and transformed by his architect, Sylvie, into a split-level mezzanine area for his office space and bedroom.

**OPPOSITE** The large factory trolleys have been strategically placed to create a corner effect in the main open-plan area of the apartment. Their heavy metal and wood design and visual magnitude make a foil for the soft, cocooning aesthetic of the sofa.

**FAR LEFT** Succulents and leafy houseplants provide splashes of green among Sam's burgeoning collections of vintage curios.

**LEFT** The scale and positioning of artwork need careful consideration in a small space. A painting of an elegant woman sits comfortably in the open-plan interior, creating a serene contrast to the large-scale industrial pieces.

# LOFTY ASPIRATIONS APPLYING A ROBUST FACTORY-STYLE INDUSTRIAL AESTHETIC TO A RELATIVELY SMALL INTERIOR SPACE – JUST 100 METRES/1076 FEET SQUARE – MIGHT NOT SEEM THE MOST OBVIOUS DESIGN CHOICE. HOWEVER, IN THIS TOP-FLOOR APARTMENT IN THE HEART OF THE SWEDISH CITY OF MALMO, IT HAS PROVED TO BE SOMEWHAT OF A SAVING GRACE.

The top floor of this historic, late-19th-century residential building was originally designated the servants' quarters. Compromised by the structure of the building – low ceilings, due to the constraints of the roof space, and three chimneys running through the apartment, with two on the walls at opposite ends and one right in the middle – and with a useful back stairwell, it would have originally been home to just a tiny kitchen, laundry room and living space for a maid. With windows being mostly limited to the front of the building to maintain the consistency of the façade, it was clearly constructed with thought to practicality rather than

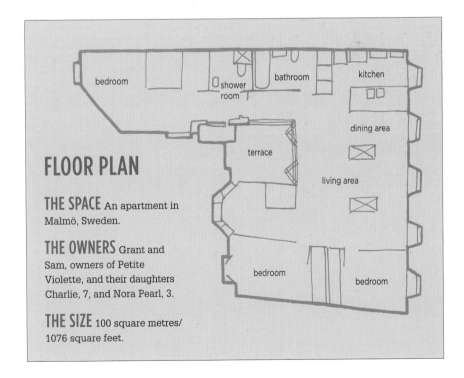

## FLOOR PLAN

**THE SPACE** An apartment in Malmö, Sweden.

**THE OWNERS** Grant and Sam, owners of Petite Violette, and their daughters Charlie, 7, and Nora Pearl, 3.

**THE SIZE** 100 square metres/ 1076 square feet.

**ABOVE** For someone who favours industrial-style furniture, living in a small space is very challenging. Despite Sam's love of collecting, every single item brought into the apartment has been carefully considered to avoid cluttering the place.

**OPPOSITE** A pair of well-worn comfortable leather armchairs sit side by side in a symmetrical fashion that gives them an air of purpose and helps to create an aura of calm.

convenience, and was certainly never designed to be a lavish living space, nor one that could accommodate a family and all their possessions. More recent modifications had further 'shrunk' the space, with rooms crammed around the various structural obstacles and resulting in a confusing layout with little head height or usable floor space.

But for Grant and Sam, drawn to the space by the charm of the architectural aesthetic of the old building and its central location – just minutes away from school, daycare, their work places and the vibrant cafés and restaurants of the old town area – and despite the fact

that many of their friends were moving out of the city to larger houses once they had children, it instinctively felt like the right place to make a home. With an already burgeoning collection of rescued, renovated and revamped ex-industrial and salvaged pieces, many of which have been put into service as fabulous storage options, it seemed appropriate to create a space that was nicely open plan and spatially appropriate for relaxed family living. However, they also wanted to retain as much of the original character of the interior as possible so that it could serve as a suitable backdrop for their miscellany.

Clearly needing to tick all the boxes from a practical perspective – three bedrooms, a bathroom that doubled as a utility room, a small south-facing terrace and a kitchen/dining/living area that would make up the heart of the apartment – it was imperative that Sam and Grant utilize absolutely every inch of space. Their initial thoughts included a mezzanine level, to maximize the space they would gain by exposing the beams, but they decided that it would be too imposing and inhibit the flow of the apartment. Instead, they decided to focus on the aesthetic potential of the interior and work with the existing floor space. They did, however, build a clever little 'cubby-house' on top of the two wardrobes that are on either side of the wall that separates the girls' bedrooms. With its own door, and accessible from the living room via a ladder, it will provide additional storage when no longer used as a den by the girls.

**LEFT** To make the kitchen a 'separate room' within the open-plan space, the couple installed a large stainless-steel island bench between the dining and kitchen areas. It is big enough to incorporate sink, drawers, cupboards, dishwasher, rubbish bin, freezer and microwave. The natural brick wall also provides a visual partition from the rest of the interior.

**RIGHT** A hanging rail for utensils makes the most of the generous depth of the kitchen window. The sill offers a shelf for pots of herbs and gadgets.

**BELOW RIGHT** A small factory trolley is the perfect space-saving storage alternative to wall-mounted, door-fronted kitchen cabinets. The stacks of china and glassware create a wealth of visual interest too.

"THE LARGE STAINLESS-STEEL ISLAND ACTS AS A BREAK BETWEEN THE DINING AND KITCHEN AREAS. I DON'T THINK THAT PEOPLE SHOULD BE SCARED OF USING SOMETHING BIG IN A SMALL SPACE, JUST AS LONG AS IT COMPLEMENTS THE SPACE AND DOES NOT TAKE OVER."

**ABOVE LEFT** A collection of old boxes and large tins rests on a freestanding wardrobe in the couple's bedroom. This form of storage is both practical and aesthetically appealing.

**ABOVE RIGHT** Finding storage solutions is an evolutionary process that owes much to the couple's love of collecting vintage pieces. A rescued rack of drawers in the bedroom alcove now houses Grant's office paperwork.

The remodelling was quite extensive: walls were knocked down, a chimney breast removed and a large section of the roof was torn down and built up and out to increase the floor space and ceiling height of the apartment. The floor was levelled, skylights were added and the windows suitably positioned to maximize light – this is Sweden, after all, and small attic apartments need to have as much light as possible to make the space feel capacious, especially in the winter. The ceilings were removed and the beams in the roof were exposed to give the apartment some much-needed height

and a sense of space. It also, somewhat unintentionally, provided a clever and quirky storage solution, as the framework of the beams created 'shelving' for industrial-style aluminium crates that are stuffed with all sorts of bits and pieces.

This is a cleverly constructed interior that has been allowed to maintain a strong sense of history despite its relatively compact size and the extent of the remodelling of the space. The successful results are entirely due to the couple's considered and intelligent design planning and their sympathetic approach to renovation.

"WE WANTED TO MAXIMIZE THE ENTIRE FLOOR SPACE, INCREASE THE LIGHT AND AIR FLOW AND GIVE THE APARTMENT THE APPEARANCE OF BEING LARGER BY TEARING DOWN THE CEILINGS AND EXPOSING THE LARGE WOODEN BEAMS THAT THEY CONCEALED."

**THIS PAGE** The off-white shade chosen for the walls in the bedroom, and throughout the apartment, complements the honey tones of the vintage wooden pieces and the exposed beams. The polished-steel radiators are both functional and beautiful, as well as adding atmosphere to the apartment.

**ABOVE LEFT** The compact apartment has two bathrooms, a small ensuite that leads off the couple's bedroom and a larger one used by the whole family. Despite the shower room's diminutive proportions, it has been given a touch of grandeur by the addition of traditional sanitaryware and some pretty accessories.

**LEFT** A structural ventilation shaft that couldn't be moved created a less-than-desirable layout in one of the girls' bedrooms. To overcome this problem, a single bed was placed on one side by the window and a desk, with storage above, on the other.

**ABOVE RIGHT** Both bathrooms have sliding barn doors, since normal doors would have taken up too much space. The design aesthetic of each is in keeping with the overall industrial style, while white Metro tiles and black grouting provide a utilitarian feel.

The formidable beams, and the exposed brickwork in the kitchen provide a sense of drama and are complemented by other utilitarian classics, such as the factory lighting, the stainless-steel worktops and the sizeable Smeg fridge. But the eye is offered visual contrast in the shape of the simple elegance of the vintage, pastel-painted cupboard-cum-pantry and the display of utensils hanging across the kitchen window.

In the connecting dining space, 'Tolix' chairs are softened by a time-worn, scrubbed-top wooden table, and similarly in the living area, the couple's collection of wooden and metal vintage storage trolleys, piled high with magazines, books and other paraphernalia, are balanced effortlessly by the cloud-like, comfy white couch.

Sam has an excellent eye for detail and has incorporated many items in a seamless and coherent style that enhances the aesthetic and makes this compact family home a warm and lively space without it feeling cluttered. Dotted around the place, on windowsills and shelves, are decorative arrangements that provide the eye with respite from the larger-scale pieces and industrial feel of the rest of the space, giving it a sense of calm and an immense feeling of cosiness.

"WE HAVE USED SLIDING BARN DOORS ON THE BATHROOM AND EN SUITE, AS NORMAL DOORS WOULD HAVE TAKEN UP TOO MUCH SPACE."

**THIS PAGE** An arrangement of vintage kitchen items – milk bottle, pastry moulds and cooling tray – makes up one of several cameos and vignettes of exquisitely tiny objects that offer a playful contrast of scale with the larger industrial pieces.

**OPPOSITE** A simple-to-construct partition wall screens off the part of the kitchen area allocated to cooking and washing so that it is out of view from the rest of the open-plan space. A pair of stackable stools keeps the space feeling airy.

**FAR LEFT** Stylist Saša was inspired by the shade of blue of his favourite cashmere scarf when deciding on the colour for the kitchen units, so he took the scarf with him to the paint store to find a match.

**LEFT** Small but effective, this tiny wall mirror reflects a splash of bright blue from the kitchen cabinets.

# WONDERWALL

SOMETIMES THE SMALLEST IDEAS HAVE THE BIGGEST IMPACT, AND IN THE CASE OF THIS COMPACT STUDIO IN THE HEART OF STOCKHOLM, THE INGENUITY OF ITS CREATIVE OWNER HAS PROVED TO BE ITS MOST VALUABLE ASSET. AN INTERIOR OF MINUSCULE PROPORTIONS, STRETCHING TO JUST 24 SQUARE METRES/258 SQUARE FEET, HAS BEEN AFFORDED A DECEPTIVE FEELING OF SPACE, THANKS TO A COUPLE OF SIMPLE MODIFICATIONS.

Set in the central Södermalm district of the city, on the picturesque island of the same name and in what is one of the most densely populated parts of the Swedish capital, this former working-class area of Stockholm has become gentrified over the years. It is now an increasingly popular neighbourhood. Abbreviated to SoFo for short, it attracts all sorts, from bohemian and artistic types to some of the city's most successful professionals, and with its quaint streets interspersed with small shops, artisan studios and a wealth of cultural amenities, it's easy to see why apartments of any size are becoming increasingly more expensive and difficult to come by.

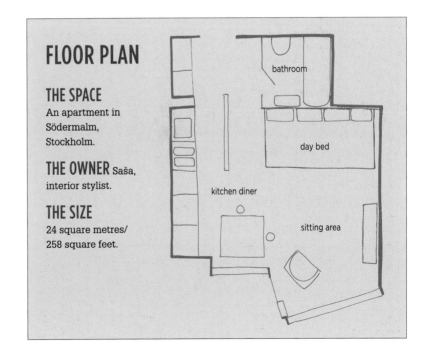

## FLOOR PLAN

### THE SPACE
An apartment in Södermalm, Stockholm.

### THE OWNER Saša,
interior stylist.

### THE SIZE
24 square metres/ 258 square feet.

bathroom

day bed

kitchen diner

sitting area

For stylist and self-confessed 'city slicker' Saša, the apartment is minutes away from friends and his work studio, and in an area packed with valuable creative inspiration. Totally won over by the location, which is, as he puts it, 'in the middle of everything', and with a balcony just large enough for a table and a couple of chairs, the compact size of the studio was an acceptable compromise. From his little piece of outside space, one is offered a view down the hill and over the water to some of Stockholm's most picture-postcard-perfect scenery

While small, the apartment has an exceptionally light-filled interior, due in part to the wall-to-wall bank of windows and patio doors that front the building, but also thanks to Saša's imaginative approach. Despite its original shabby state – the flat had been rented out prior to the purchase and was in desperate need of a refit, with tatty and overly flamboyant wallpaper everywhere – it was clear that a couple of clever modifications could make the one-room set-up suitable for permanent living.

With no spare height in the ceilings to capitalize on, since there is another floor of apartments above, a mezzanine or attic conversion was out of the question. The space consisted of a tiny hallway leading off to a small but

**ABOVE** The partition wall is a success on the kitchen side, offering a thoroughfare to the hallway. The slimline shelves provide much-needed storage for ceramics and glassware, and a mirrored wall at the far end reflects daylight into this corner of the studio, enhancing the feeling of space.

**RIGHT** As a stylist and lover of beautiful homewares, Saša has utilized his styling and display skills to great effect, creating little pockets of visual interest by the arrangement of the items on the shelves.

"THE SIMPLEST WAY OF ENLIVENING A COMPACT SPACE IS TO BRING IN AN ELEMENT OF NATURE, JUST SOMETHING SMALL AND SIMPLE, SUCH AS A BEAUTIFUL BRANCH, ONE GORGEOUS FLOWER OR EVEN A FEATHER YOU FOUND ON THE STREET."

**THIS PAGE** Simple vertical shelving displaying sculptural ceramics leads the eye upward, creating a sense of height, while a table weighed down by piles of books in varying configurations, frames and other curios makes a bountiful feast for the eye in a very compact space.

"I WANTED IT TO BE A PERSONAL AND CREATIVE SPACE. I ALSO WANT TO BE ABLE TO REFRESH IT ALL THE TIME – MY STILL-LIFE MARBLE TRAY IS A COLLECTION OF BEAUTIFUL, PERSONAL THINGS THAT WORK TOGETHER AND KEEPS ON CHANGING ALL THE TIME."

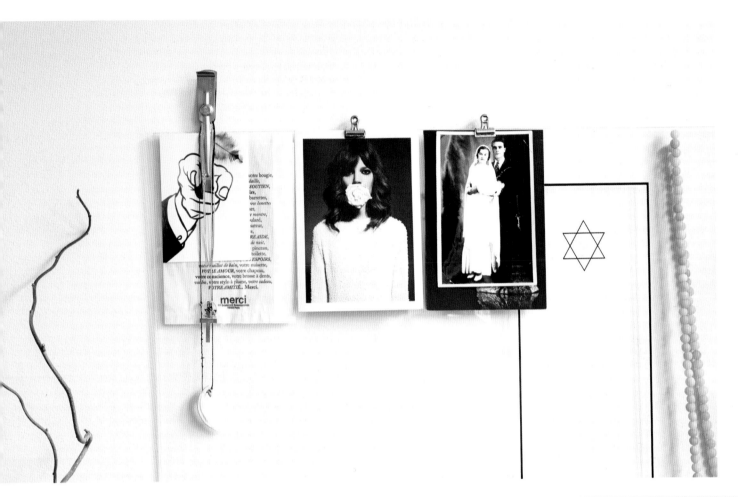

adequately sized bathroom, and a separate tiny kitchen off the main room. It is evident from the finished result that Saša has used classic decorating tricks to good effect by choosing a light-enhancing pure white for the walls, but teaming it with a contrast colour – a soft olive green – on the ceiling that cleverly 'canopies' the open-plan room and accentuates its length.

However, the key element of this space is the partition wall that Saša and a builder friend added between the newly fitted galley kitchen and the living space. This was a relatively straightforward and cost-effective exercise, but one that has had huge impact by effectively segregating the working part of the kitchen – the cooking and washing-up areas – from the main part of the studio room without losing the open-plan feel. It also creates a thoroughfare between the hallway and kitchen, providing a welcome

**OPPOSITE** Saša's collection of books is his biggest inspiration. Their graphic qualities and coloured spines echo the stripes and patterns in his textiles.

**ABOVE** A simple piece of Perspex sheeting has been transformed into a display board for photos, postcards and personal mementos that can easily be changed for an instant update.

**LEFT** Saša has created a charmingly impromptu and super-stylish coffee table from a simple pile of books.

flow between the different areas. The floor-to-ceiling mirror that covers the partition wall further enhances the effect of space, bouncing light around the living space, and making it appear larger than it is. On the kitchen side, Saša has designed long, thin shelves that function both as storage and display space for pieces of kitchen equipment and tableware that are as decorative as they are useful, adding another layer of visual interest to the tiny space.

"I LOVE THINGS, BUT I DIDN'T WANT THE SPACE TO FEEL CROWDED, WHILE ON THE OTHER HAND I DIDN'T WANT IT TO LOOK STERILE AND COLD. IT'S A FINE BALANCE."

**OPPOSITE, ABOVE**
Inspired by displays in local galleries, Saša has created his own studio-style collection of artisan pots and handmade bowls.

**OPPOSITE, BELOW**
Saša believes that no space is too small to be made attractive – hence the intricate displays of groups of objects thoroughout the studio.

**LEFT** The owner's love of mixing pattern and colour as a way of personalizing a home is evident in the living space. An art wall consists of framed prints of graphic stripes and blocks in unifying shades of blue, earthy neutrals and sharp black and white. These designs are repeated in the rug and the textiles on the daybed.

Of course, being a stylist, Saša has tapped deep into his wealth of knowledge and design expertise to create a feeling of space. Throughout the interior there is a carefully considered palette of his favourite colours and patterns – bold graphic prints, striped textiles, earthy shades and sculptural shapes – that seamlessly ties the individual areas together with a sense of restrained orderliness, providing visual warmth but without too much clutter. There are also some delightful display ideas, from a pile of hardback books that double up as a side table, to magpie collections of unusual, well-loved objects and curiosities that are displayed in a way more akin to a gallery, and which are constantly updated to keep this pretty little space looking suitably stylish and suitably refreshed.

**RIGHT** A long rectangular glass aperture allows daylight to enter from the dining room into the otherwise dark bathroom located on the other side of the wall.

**FAR RIGHT** An inexpensive way to add bursts of colour is to invest in some budget-friendly accessories such as rice bowls and plastic chopsticks.

**OPPOSITE** Colour is an invaluable tool for adding personality and energy to a small interior. Here, a vibrant shade of blue has been used to draw the eye down and away from the apartment's sloping eaves.

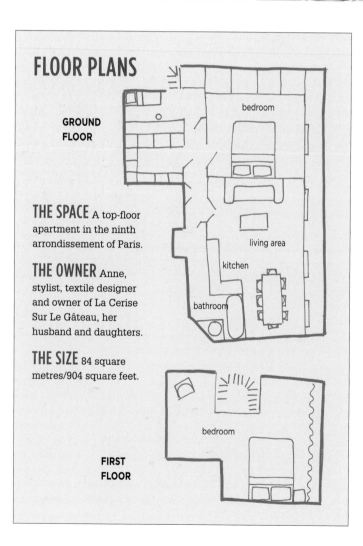

## FLOOR PLANS

**GROUND FLOOR**

bedroom

**THE SPACE** A top-floor apartment in the ninth arrondissement of Paris.

**THE OWNER** Anne, stylist, textile designer and owner of La Cerise Sur Le Gâteau, her husband and daughters.

**THE SIZE** 84 square metres/904 square feet.

living area

kitchen

bathroom

bedroom

**FIRST FLOOR**

# COLOURFUL AND CREATIVE AN UNASSUMING ENTRANCE ON THE STREET DOES LITTLE TO PREPARE THE VISITOR FOR WHAT LIES AT THE TOP OF THIS TRADITIONAL APARTMENT BLOCK IN THE HEART OF THE NINTH ARRONDISSEMENT OF THE FRENCH CAPITAL. BUT THROUGH THE WOODEN DOOR, PAST THE COMMUNAL HALLWAY AND UP THE STEEP WINDING STAIRCASE IS THE COLOURFUL AND CREATIVE CITY PIED A TERRE OF TEXTILE DESIGNER ANNE AND HER FAMILY.

This petite sixth-floor Parisian apartment is blessed with a natural charm, thanks to the sloping ceilings that are part of the mansard-style roof. These are beautifully balanced by the lofty and elegantly proportioned floor-to-ceiling French windows, which open out onto a chic, wrought-iron balcony that runs the entire length of the front of the apartment building.

"THE KITCHEN IS A PRACTICAL SPACE. IT'S SMALL, LIKE A DOLL'S HOUSE, BUT IT WORKS. THE LAYOUT IS COMPACT BUT EASY TO USE."

**LEFT** The kitchen is a warm and homely space with natural wood surfaces and a window that allows plenty of natural light to enter. Anne's own designs – the fabric utensil holders and brightly patterned dish towels – add a colourful touch of whimsical charm.

**BELOW LEFT** A random selection of objects in assorted sizes, from huge lettering to a minuscule teacup, creates an eye-catching display in this creative home.

**BELOW RIGHT** Anne had the low-level storage unit built to her specifications. The compartments are designed to be the optimum height for storing her burgeoning collection of interior and lifestyle magazines and books. The bright blue, one of her favourite colours, is picked up in other furniture and decorative pieces throughout the apartment.

The deep navy painted hallway of the apartment provides the first glimpse into this creative and colourful space, and illustrates beautifully the impact gained from using a dark shade in a small space. The rich blue brings a luxurious elegance to what might otherwise feel like a gloomy and cramped space. It also serves as a fabulous contrast to the various bright and airy rooms flooded with natural light that lead off it.

Once a dark space with carpeted floors and papered walls, Anne has transformed the interior of the apartment through decoration alone. Being a lover of light and bright spaces,

and recognizing the abundance of natural daylight that was available, Anne decided to use it to her advantage. She painted all the walls of the main rooms white to give a feeling of spaciousness to the small space, but treated some of the floors to colourful hues – sky blue in the living room and a leafy green upstairs – that effectively anchor the walls and draw the eye down and away from the confinement of the low ceilings.

Anne also infused each room with her favourite palette of neon shades, with spots of pink and red in the rugs and an intriguing collection of furnishings, textiles and personal

**ABOVE** The living area is a haven of comfort and fun – testament to Anne's creativity, not to mention her former life as a stylist. As well as the set of old school chairs around the dining table, Anne has unearthed some fabulous vintage finds at flea markets, including the supersized old shop signage and standard lamp. An assortment of her own cushion designs is piled high on the sofa.

**THIS PAGE** Anne's home is typical of many top-floor Parisian apartments. Its charming sloping ceilings are formed by the mansard roof, and Anne has utilized this to great effect by positioning an antique chair of tiny proportions underneath.

*La bonnerie*

**FAR LEFT** The soft taupe of Anne's big squashy sofa is the perfect backdrop to the riot of pattern and colour in her cushion designs. Fluorescent pinks, pastels and florals all mix together for an eclectic and hugely personal style.

**LEFT** Anne uses the apartment for work and a spare corner has been transformed into a compact home office. A neat row of storage boxes and drawers is ideal for keeping the tiny spot tidy.

**BELOW** The intense blue that Anne has selected for the hallway is ideally suited to a naturally dark corridor that is starved of natural light.

objects. The apartment, which stretches upwards into the roof space by way of a tiny staircase to a second bedroom and dressing area, is a perfect example of how fresh white teamed with splashes of pattern and colour can enliven and re-energize the low proportions and architectural quirks of an old and compact space.

The apartment embodies the quintessential romantic Parisian loft, with views from the elegant windows over the rooftops of the city skyline which, when combined with Anne's natural style and creative and playful approach to the décor, makes this small space deliver both on a practical and aesthetic level. The open-plan living/dining area offers a sense of space, but the room's restricted head space by the windows creates cosy corners that in turn dictate furniture choices. A delicately proportioned armchair sits beneath the eaves, and a deep, low sofa provides all the comfort necessary without feeling cramped.

Anne has cleverly played with proportions, creating a doll's house effect by juxtaposing small and low pieces with tall, skinny standard lamps and oversized lettering on the wall. Dainty school-style dining chairs provide a contrast in proportion to the large yellow-topped wooden table,

**ABOVE LEFT** The main bedroom is colourful and creative, in keeping with Anne's signature style. A rectangular block of fluorescent yellow paint on the wall behind the bed is a cost-effective and a simple-to-achieve alternative to a headboard.

**ABOVE CENTRE** This unusual light fitting is ideal for a small bedroom. Its simple wire structure, which has also been given a coat of bright yellow, allows the eye to see straight through to the block of blue behind.

**ABOVE RIGHT** It pays to think laterally when furnishing small spaces. A tiny vintage kitchen table has been transformed into a dressing table with an old junk shop mirror and repainted dining chair.

creating a sense of easy intimacy when just one or two people are eating, but also providing ample seating for sociable gatherings.

Anne's ideas are simple but effective and hark back to the days when she worked as a stylist and was decorating her first home on a limited budget. This apartment certainly still pays homage to her frugal former life, with the washing line of postcards and notes pegged above one of the beds, and the headboard created out of a painted section of the wall. In the second bedroom, Anne has made an impromptu clothes rail from lengths of bamboo and customized it with a splash of fluorescent pink, creating the perfect storage solution for a space unable to

accommodate a large wardrobe. Bookshelves are slotted into a tiny slimline alcove at the edge of this room, and the low space under the eaves has been transformed into a storage area that's screened off by a simple curtain.

With a family home in the countryside, the flat is very much a city crash pad for the family and a working space for Anne, inspiring some of her designs. Her whimsical, floral and colourful tongue-in-cheek textiles are reminiscent of the quirkiness and naivety of childhood, and are designed around her philosophy that 'normal is boring', so it seems appropriate that this little city hideaway, with its characterful period details and nooks and crannies, is the home for all that creative ingenuity.

**THIS PAGE** A wall of storage with doors of different sizes in varying tones of turquoise dominates this tiny room. The doors are fitted with push-pull latches for a clean aesthetic. Anne's bold black and white polka dot bed linen provides a welcome contrast.

**THIS PAGE** The charm of Anne's flat comes very much from the restrictions imposed by the structure and natural shape of the roof. Original beams are characterful and have been left exposed to create a cosy nook for the guest bed. The natural space created under the eaves has been fully utilized and turned into storage with a simple curtain to screen off the contents.

"I CHOSE THIS APARTMENT PRIMARILY FOR THE LIGHT AND QUIETNESS, AND FOR THE CHARM OF A ROOM UNDER THE ROOFS OF PARIS! I WANTED TO FIND A PLACE WHERE I COULD FEEL COSY AND COCOONED."

**BELOW LEFT** Every inch has been put to good use in this old apartment. A triangular slice of empty wall at the side of the sloping roof has been turned into storage for books.

**BELOW RIGHT** Despite its diminutive size and lack of natural daylight, the bathroom has a lovely fresh feel. Anne has chosen a cement grey colour for most of the space, complemented with a fresh zesty lime on one wall, and towel hooks in fuchsia pink.

**RIGHT** The height of the attic is too low for a conventional wardrobe, which would be heavy and cumbersome in the small space, and block out valuable daylight too. Anne has constructed a charming and impromptu clothes rail out of rickety bamboo canes, the shape of which echoes that of the beams. Her love of colour is as evident in her clothes as in the décor of the apartment.

**RIGHT** Appliances specifically designed for compact interios have been used to good effect, allowing the tiny kitchen to be a fully functioning cooking area. There is even room for a space-saving drawer dishwasher.

**FAR RIGHT** The structural beams create natural partition walls between the kitchen and the bathroom beyond.

**OPPOSITE** The triangular apex of the roof space and natural low ceilings dictate the layout of the studio. The architect has designed the different areas according to the amount of head height each requires, to maximize the space's potential.

# CHIC PETITE WHILE THIS PINT-SIZED PAD IN THE SIXTH ARRONDISSEMENT OF PARIS CERTAINLY SHOWS WHAT CAN BE ACHIEVED WITH EVEN THE MOST DIMINUTIVE AND AWKWARD OF SPACES, IT ALSO SERVES AS A STARK REMINDER OF THE COST OF INNER-CITY LIVING, AND THE IMPACT ON AFFORDABILITY OF A MUCH SOUGHT-AFTER LOCATION.

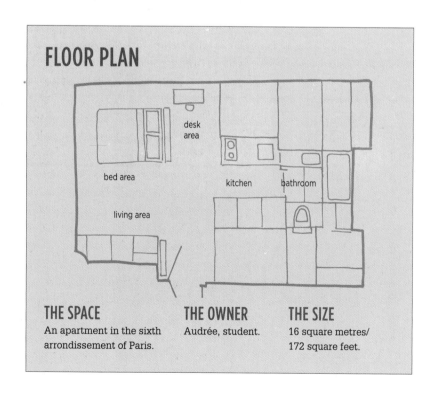

## FLOOR PLAN

desk area

bed area

kitchen    bathroom

living area

## THE SPACE
An apartment in the sixth arrondissement of Paris.

## THE OWNER
Audrée, student.

## THE SIZE
16 square metres/ 172 square feet.

Situated in the heart of St-Germain-des-Prés, a fashionable central Paris district that's home to many of France's intellectual and artistic thinkers, this tiny studio lies just minutes away from the boutiques, restaurants and cafés of Boulevard St Germain – a highly desirable part of the Left Bank where property comes with a somewhat less-than-desirable price tag.

While its suitability, defined by its size, is clearly limited to sole occupancy, for its owner Audrée, a student at the Sorbonne, it is perfect. Situated just a few minutes' walk away from the university and the Jardins du Luxembourg, it is in close proximity to an abundance of lively and popular cafés, including Parisian institutions such as Les Deux Magots and Café de Flore.

AUDRÉE: "THIS PLACE WAS PERFECT FOR ME, AS I AM NOT TOO TALL. IT IS IDEAL FOR A STUDENT LIVING ALONE...IT IS PRACTICAL TO LIVE IN; TO SLEEP, TO EAT, WORK, ETC."

**OPPOSITE** The apartment has several large Velux windows that allow daylight to flood into the various spaces. The light-wood flooring and white walls have been chosen to accentuate the impression of space.

**LEFT** Audrée's furniture choices are perfect for such a small space. A light-reflective glass-topped dining table doubles as a desk, and can be extended in size when required. The Perspex/plexiglass chair and stools, sometimes used as side tables, are airy in feel.

**BELOW** Due to the studio's awkward size and shape, the only way to accommodate cupboards was to have them custom-built. Two full-height ones are for Audrée's clothes and shoes, while a run of smaller ones are ideal for student files and books.

Despite its small size, the space delivers on both practicality and style. The compact apartment is kitted out with all mod cons and offers everything needed for student living: a desk – which doubles as a dining table – and plenty of storage. While the space doesn't allow for a great deal of privacy nor a separate bedroom – a low-level couch is also the bed – this in itself provides an appropriately bohemian feel to the place, and seems a fitting backdrop to Parisian student life.

The original space, at the time just attic storage in what is a historic 17th-century building, provided architect Sylvie Cahen with something of a challenge. The existing structure of the sharply pitched roof with its low supporting beams couldn't be altered, and so it dictated the layout to a large extent. The solution was to create clearly defined living spaces, determined by the amount of head height each one required. The central part of the space, which offered the most height, was reserved for standing activities (showering, cooking and

**ABOVE** Sylvie, the architect, has utilized the structure of the beam to create a barrier between the lounging/sleeping area and the rest of the space. It also makes a shelf for a table lamp and tealight holders.

**ABOVE RIGHT** The rafters that form part of the structure of the sharply pitched roof create some interesting angles, as well as little 'windows' that make it possible to look right through the space, enhancing the sense of openness.

**OPPOSITE** Without space for a separate bedroom, Audrée has incorporated a low-level daybed that doubles as a bed for sleeping in at the opposite end of the studio from the kitchen and bathroom. It is furnished with pillows and cushions in her restrained pink, grey and red colour palette. The low bed and the architectural structure of the space create an almost cathedral-like loftiness.

walking), while the sides, with restricted height, were allotted to sleeping and storage space, leaving the intermediate areas for sitting activities such as eating or studying.

The open-plan layout was intentional; its sole purpose to keep everything within reach and sight, thereby maximizing the sense of space. The original windows were removed and their positions altered to increase the amount of natural light – and successfully so, because, despite its minuscule proportions, this really is an incredibly light-filled space. Sylvie points out that the apartment feels connected to the sky, as the views extend up and over the Parisian skyline and the tower of Saint-Sulpice church to the clouds beyond.

Sylvie further enhanced the luminosity of the interior with a considered choice of materials and colours. Clean whites play a major part, complemented by a subtle but clever

SYLVIE: "I WANTED TO CREATE A FLUID SPACE WITH A MULTI-FUNCTIONAL QUALITY. FOR EXAMPLE, THE DINING AREA BETWEEN THE SLEEPING SPACE AND THE KITCHEN CAN ALSO BE USED AS AN OFFICE AND WORK SPACE."

**OPPOSITE AND BELOW** The dark grey colour scheme allows the shower space to recede almost out of sight when viewed from the other end of the room. Every piece of space has been used, with a tiny alcove built in for soaps and lotions, and a recessed bench area for storing towels.

**RIGHT** A cantina-style door creates sufficient privacy between the bathroom and the rest of the interior.

**BELOW RIGHT** An appropriately small sink has been inset into a bathroom cabinet, which matches the cabinets in the kitchen for a seamless visual transition between the two spaces.

range of tonal shades of white and grey. The dark grey bathroom is visually distinct from the rest of the predominantly white space and recedes nicely out of sight from the opposite end of the room. The incredibly compact but fully functioning kitchen has been furnished with white high-gloss units and light-reflective work surfaces, which add to the sense of space. The whitewashed oak flooring and white-painted walls and beams further emphasize this, and are broken only by tiny splashes of colour in the form of accessories and textiles. Furniture has been carefully chosen, with an extendable table and a 'see-through' Perspex/plexiglass chair and coordinating stacking stools.

For Audrée, this tiny apartment is the perfect little home. Both pretty and practical, it offers just enough space for entertaining and relaxing with a few friends once their studies are done.

**OPPOSITE** The Bridget Riley 'Rose, Rose' Olympic print above the fireplace was chosen because of its similarity to seaside and nautical stripes. Its contemporary and colourful design also introduces a playful element to the otherwise minimal and rustic aesthetic of the dining room.

**FAR LEFT** The delicate ironwork and dainty structure of a vintage shelving unit makes it the perfect storage solution for the small room.

**LEFT** A couple of suitably small old school chairs make great extra seating, as they can be stacked neatly in the alcove when not in use. Their utilitarian style is ideal for this former worker's cottage.

# FLOTSAM AND JETSAM SET AMONG THE WINDSWEPT DUNES OF THE WILD, FLAT COASTAL LANDSCAPE OF EAST SUSSEX, THIS VICTORIAN TERRACED HOUSE WAS ORIGINALLY AS UTILITARIAN IN ITS DESIGN AS IT WAS IN ITS PURPOSE. A FORMER COASTGUARD'S COTTAGE, ITS INTERIOR CONSISTED OF A HANDFUL OF TINY ROOMS — A CELLAR, TWO ROOMS DOWNSTAIRS AND THREE SMALLER ROOMS ABOVE — AND A CENTRAL CONCEALED STAIRCASE HIDDEN BEHIND A DOOR.

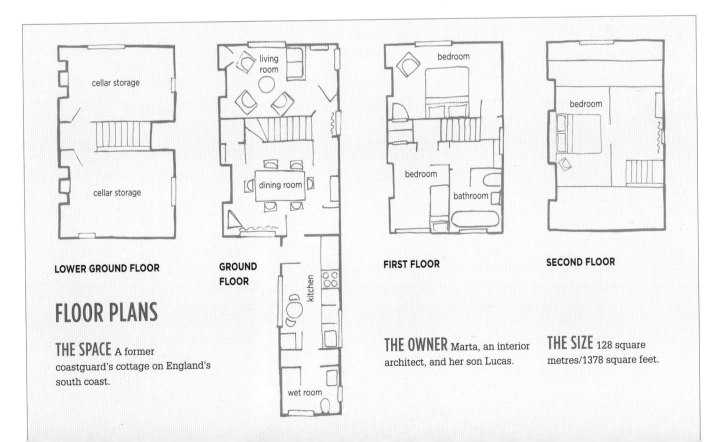

**LOWER GROUND FLOOR**

cellar storage

cellar storage

**GROUND FLOOR**

living room

dining room

kitchen

wet room

**FIRST FLOOR**

bedroom

bedroom

bathroom

**SECOND FLOOR**

bedroom

bedroom

## FLOOR PLANS

**THE SPACE** A former coastguard's cottage on England's south coast.

**THE OWNER** Marta, an interior architect, and her son Lucas.

**THE SIZE** 128 square metres/1378 square feet.

"SMALLER SPACES TEND TO BE EASIER TO LIVE IN, AS ALL THE ACTIVITIES HAPPEN IN A CONDENSED SPACE!"

The compact size of the cottage is, of course, historical and has purpose, with its small rooms and internal layout enabling the house to retain as much warmth as possible, and offering maximum protection and respite from the battering winds that blow in from the sea. While modern times have introduced modern methods of heating and modern ways of living — Marta and her son divide their time between the cottage and their busy lives and Marta's design business in London — the original aesthetic has been carefully preserved. The house still retains the same layout, with its charming, enclosed 'secret' staircase and small rooms with simple, understated period features, and it is this combination that makes this small space work so beautifully. It still offers its residents the perfect safe haven and retreat, but this time from the stresses of city life rather than the constantly changing seascape outside the window.

**LEFT** The rustic wooden table that takes centre stage in the dining room is evidence of Marta's love of weather-beaten textures and materials. The vintage Ernest Race 'Antelope' chairs are graceful and compact thanks to their steel wire design, making them perfect for small spaces.

**RIGHT** Creative storage enhances the personality of a small interior. Here, a salvaged door hung on the wall serves as a hat and coat stand.

**BELOW RIGHT** An extension to the dining room houses the new kitchen. It has a clean, uncluttered industrial aesthetic that respects the history of this former worker's cottage, but it has been fitted with all modern conveniences in utilitarian stainless steel.

The changes to the original footprint of the building are sympathetic add-ons. An extension/addition to the dining room is home to the kitchen, which displays a clean, practical, industrial design that makes reference to the original functionality of the house but contains all the necessary mod cons. The other extension in this compact house is an upwards one into the eaves, where otherwise redundant attic space has been transformed into a characterful bedroom. Accessed via a narrow, nautical-style wooden

staircase tucked into a corner of the first-floor landing, the bedroom continues the sense of intimacy and protection provided by the layout of the rest of the house. With styling clearly influenced by its maritime connections — the rafters of the roof space have been clad in horizontal tongue and groove reminiscent of a ship's interior and painted white — it is a sleeping space that is as unique as it is desirable.

Throughout the house, there is a strong sense of connection between the interior and its coastal location. Collections of pebbles and shells brought home after walks along the beach are dotted around the house, and there is much evidence of Marta's love of weather-beaten textures and materials and of the beauty that exists in nature itself.

As part of the extensive renovations – the house was bought as a complete wreck – the floorboards were stripped, sanded and left bare, as were areas of brickwork around some of the fireplaces. The interior walls were painstakingly stripped back to the original plaster, revealing the exquisite hues of the natural pigments which, on first inspection, might be taken for a creative paint effect. A bare plaster wall in the dining room reveals a palette of soft shades of oyster pink, while upstairs in the bedroom a mottled soft gold tone, which could easily be mistaken as an interior designer's

**ABOVE** Marta took down a suspended ceiling in the kitchen to create a light and airy feel to the room. Little nooks and crannies such as the one above the door (which was created by adding a partition shelf to the roof space) give small spaces character, as well as providing storage.

**RIGHT** Open shelves stacked with everyday crockery, pots, pans and other cooking essentials are made into even more of a visual feast with the addition of a couple of small but personal pictures.

"WITH LOTS OF SMALL ROOMS YOU DON'T GET ON TOP OF EACH OTHER AND THERE'S ALWAYS A QUIET SPACE TO RETREAT TO."

**THIS PAGE** In the living room, a clever combination of sizes, shapes and textures creates a welcoming and relaxed vibe. To avoid the room becoming too cluttered, and for an extra feeling of intimacy, Marta opted for individual chairs but in different shapes and styles.

"IT'S AN EASY HOME TO LIVE IN AS IT'S COMPACT, THE KITCHEN IS RIGHT BY THE FRONT DOOR AND THE BEDROOMS ARE SMALL BUT SEVERAL, SO SOCIALIZING IS FUN AS EVERYONE CAN SLEEP OVER."

**LEFT** The door that opens from the dining room reveals the original staircase. Marta wanted a simplicity in keeping with the cottage's past but mixed with contextual design elements such as the rope banisters she added here.

**BELOW LEFT** Sourcing children's furniture for small spaces is straightforward, as children's rooms are often more compact. Under-bed storage can be custom-built, or you can opt for beds designed with drawers underneath.

**BELOW RIGHT** The upstairs landing is New England in style, with its white-painted wood cladding on the walls. The charming stairs and steep wooden ladder refer to the cottage's maritime connections, and lead up to a bedroom in the roof space. Marta's intention was to keep the look of the extended space as low key as possible, and she designed the stairs up to the bedroom to have a nautical, playful feel – as if one were climbing up from the galley of a boat or into a tree-house.

elaborate treatment with gold leaf, shines through and adds a luxurious decorative element to this tiny room. It might have been easier and quicker just to replaster and adorn the walls with pictures, but Marta's intention was to create an interior that was less than pristine, had a connection with its environs and allowed the imperfections and natural elements of the building to take centre stage, thereby reducing the need to clutter the compact spaces with incidental objects.

Less is often more in small spaces, and here the theory works beautifully because of the careful balance between the pared-back and unfussy interior and the incorporation of just a few essential and sensual luxuries. These include the compact but still decadently voluminous iron bathtub in the tiny bathroom, and the large rustic wooden dining table for entertaining groups of friends, teamed with a generous number of stackable dining chairs that can be neatly tucked away into an alcove when not in use. A smattering of salvaged furniture pieces and vintage finds adds interest without over-cluttering, and prevents the interior from feeling too finished or perfect, but instead one that is constantly evolving and being refreshed.

**ABOVE** The main bedroom is a lesson in how a few carefully edited pieces can result in enormous visual interest. Against a simple palette of crisp white, the shining glory of the room is without doubt the exquisite natural hue of the plaster wall – offset by a single gold-decorated glass vase on the mantelpiece. The abstract painting in muted shades also earns its place in this tiny room, as it mirrors the detail on the original fireplace.

**THIS PAGE** Marta extended upwards into the attic, converting the otherwise redundant space into a secluded and charming master bedroom.

**OPPOSITE** In the tiny bathroom, the luxuriously deep tub is scaled down in size in order to fit the space.

"THE SMALL ROOMS ARE COSY, WARM AND RELAXING, WHILE THE ATTIC SPACE FEELS LOFTY AND HAS WONDERFUL VIEWS."

**OPPOSITE** A restrained and muted palette of colours was chosen for the apartment, but this blank canvas has been injected with enlivening shots of bold red-and-yellow-coloured accessories.

**FAR LEFT** The small but perfectly formed kitchen has an abundance of carefully planned storage, offering a home for everything from bottles of wine to cookery books.

**LEFT** In the kitchen area, Armando's treasured espresso machine sits in state in a cubbyhole all of its very own, set into the middle of a wall of cupboards.

# A CLEVER CUBE THIS COMPACT, MODERN APARTMENT IS NOT ONLY A GREAT EXAMPLE OF A SMALL YET FULLY FUNCTIONAL LIVING SPACE IN A VIBRANT PART OF INNER LONDON CLOSE TO LIVELY BARS, MARKETS AND RESTAURANTS, BUT IT ALSO OFFERS A CLEVER AND INGENIOUS DESIGN SOLUTION TO WHAT WOULD OTHERWISE BE A CRAMPED AND PERHAPS UNLIVABLE SPACE.

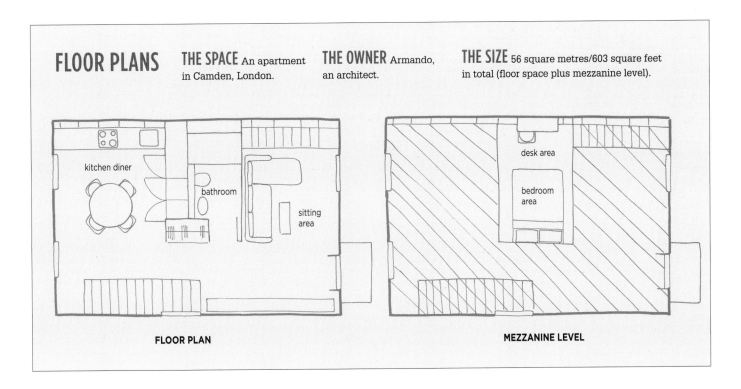

## FLOOR PLANS

**THE SPACE** An apartment in Camden, London.

**THE OWNER** Armando, an architect.

**THE SIZE** 56 square metres/603 square feet in total (floor space plus mezzanine level).

kitchen diner

bathroom

sitting area

**FLOOR PLAN**

desk area

bedroom area

**MEZZANINE LEVEL**

This diminutive space is a powerful example of what is possible with a small amount of creative thinking, the marvels of modern technology and a trained eye. It fully champions the cause for involving an architect in the remodelling of a small space in order to maximize its full potential.

For Armando, the architect behind the design, this wasn't just any small space but his own, and the one he planned on turning, together with his design practice partner Hugo, into a suitably stylish and comfortable city pad in an area of the capital that suits his social life and is just a Vespa ride away from his office too.

The apartment, situated on the top floor of a period property and once just a home office and storage space – part of a single house before it was divided into three separate units to be sold – is now an individual and innovative living space that cleverly responds to the challenges of small-space living.

**ABOVE** A slimline shelving unit recessed into the wall acts as a 'gallery space' for Armando's objects and artworks. It is regularly updated and refreshed.

**RIGHT** Armando has injected a sense of his personality into this small space with his own take on international time clocks, and a cubbyhole designed for his favourite accessory – the coffee machine.

"WE DECIDED TO GO WITH CLEAN LINES AND BRIGHT COLOURS AND, MOST IMPORTANTLY, TO INTEGRATE ALL THE APPLIANCES AND STORAGE SPACE DISCREETLY INTO THE DESIGN. THIS SIMPLICITY MADE THE SPACE FEEL MUCH BIGGER AND MORE SPACIOUS."

Upon purchase, the apartment comprised a large single room with just a toilet and sink, but the walls were covered in bookshelves, providing the architects with inspiration for the final design. While the footprint of the space was a tiny 40 square metres/430 square feet, the most defining but under-utilized features of the interior were the 4.5-metre/15-feet-high party wall and the lofty eaves, which offered Armando both height and architectural interest to work with. The challenge was to factor in every component necessary for modern living to enable the space to become an appealing one-bedroom apartment with clearly defined zones. This aim was achieved without the use of partitions, while also maximizing the overall sense of space to prevent the interior from feeling cramped and closed in.

**THIS PAGE** Four different dining chairs – a couple of classic Eames, a Verner Panton plastic stackable chair and the 'Standard' chair by Jean Prouvé – were chosen by the art-loving owner to add a sense of fun, some visual interest and a bit of iconic contemporary design to the small space.

**OPPOSITE** The use of digital fabrication allowed Armando and Hugo to save time and money in labour, as all the pieces for the storage wall were cut out off-site using CNC (computer numerical control) technologies. The plans for the design were digitally precise and took into consideration acceptable tolerances for less-than-straight walls in an old property, but nonetheless putting together the storage wall in the 1840s building was quite a challenge.

**THIS PAGE** The living space is snug, despite the high ceiling. An elegantly shaped corner sofa is covered in a tactile brushed felt and accessorized with a wool throw and rug underfoot. It is complemented by a low-level storage unit that keeps the eye level low and thus increases the sense of intimacy. Armando's large framed poster of an American roadside diner propped casually on the unit is nicely graphic, adding a dramatic statement and splash of colour.

"AS THE ORIGINAL SPACE WAS OPEN PLAN, THE INSERTION OF THE INNER BLOCK ALLOWED US TO CREATE FOUR DIFFERENT SPACES: KITCHEN-DINING, LIVING, BATHROOM AND A MEZZANINE FOR THE SLEEPING AND WORKING AREA."

**ABOVE LEFT** As well as a shower room and kitchen storage, the ingenious central cube also holds a deep closet with space for shoes and clothes.

**LEFT** The compact shower room is located beneath the double bed on the mezzanine. It feels light and bright, thanks to walls and floor covered in tiny white mosaic tiles and a feature wall of vibrant yellow.

**ABOVE** A calm and efficient work space is tucked into the gable of the roof. The desk is actually a shelf that can be folded up and clicked into place when not in use.

**OPPOSITE** The sleeping platform on top of the mezzanine is home to a double bed. The steep pitch of the roof and the skylights prevent this space from feeling claustrophic.

"BY THE TIME WE DEMOLISHED THE EXISTING LAYOUT, WE ENDED UP HAVING A BLANK CANVAS. THEN WE COULD SEE THAT THE SPACE HAD SO MUCH POTENTIAL THAT IDEAS STARTED TO COME OUT."

Armando and Hugo decided to introduce a mezzanine level to utilize the expansive ceiling space and also to divide the floor space into individual areas for living, cooking and bathing. The result is a central cube that, at ground level, appears to be a separate room, as it is detached from the façades and ceiling and 'floats' in the space, giving a sense of airiness and emphasizing the height of the overall space. The pitched lines of the eaves provided the inspiration for a staircase that leads up to the apex of the roof and the mezzanine level on top of the cube.

Inside, the cube is cleverly divided up to provide Armando with a spacious shower room and toilet, as well as closet storage and kitchen storage too, accessible from its exterior at the ground level. The mezzanine area on top of the cube is home to a low-level double bed, and at the bottom of the bed a work space occupies a niche in the wall of open storage — an additional shelf folds down and clicks into place to create an extended work surface.

A muted palette of colours has been chosen for the cube and walls, but it is punctuated with pops of bright primary shades of red and yellow in the form of details and accessories. And Armando's love of contemporary art and design adds a powerful visual punch to the apartment.

Armando has maintained a clean-lined and simple design aesthetic too, with some clever and practical touches. Push-touch latches on the cupboard doors allow the external walls of the cube to maintain a seamless visual effect that is easy on the eye in the small space. The level of the bed on top of the mezzanine has been kept deliberately low so that it can't be seen from the rest of the apartment, and the stairs blend into the wall of shelving and storage, keeping the overall effect clean and uncluttered. Tiny details, such as the small cubbyhole that houses Armando's espresso machine – his prize possession – add a sense of fun and endorse Armando's philosophy that small and compact can certainly also be clever and cool.

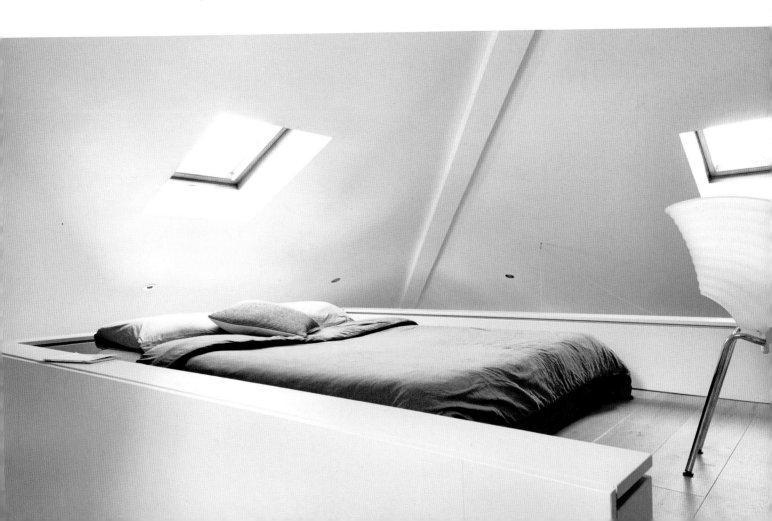

# SOURCE DIRECTORY

## UK

### USEFUL RESOURCES

**RIBA**
66 Portland Place
London W1B 1AD
+44 (0)20 7580 5533
architecture.com

*The RIBA client advisory service is a good starting point for anyone considering an architect. Also a useful online listing of all RIBA-registered practices plus contact details.*

**THE ASSOCIATION OF MASTER UPHOLSTERERS AND SOFT FURNISHERS**
The Clare Charity Centre
Wycombe Road
Saunderton
Bucks HP14 4BF
+44 (0)1494 569 120
Upholsterers.co.uk

*Listings for local trades including upholsterers, soft furnishers and furniture makers.*

**THE GUILD OF MASTER CRAFTSMEN**
166 High Street
Lewes
East Sussex BN7 1XU
Guildmc.com

*Comprehensive listing of skilled tradesmen including carpenters, builders, cabinetmakers, painters and decorators.*

### FURNITURE AND STORAGE

**ANOTHER COUNTRY**
18 Crawford Street
London W1H 1BT
+44 (0)20 7486 3251
Anothercountry.com

*Contemporary designs including multifunctional daybeds, stools and benches, plus accessories.*

**COAST TO COUNTRY**
Coast-to-country.co.uk

*Suppliers of antique bedsteads with a good selection of compact double beds.*

**THE CONRAN SHOP**
Michelin House
81 Fulham Road
London SW3 6RD
+44 (0)20 7589 7401
conranshop.co.uk

*Quality contemporary furniture, including Conran own designs and iconic designer classics, as well as a wide range of rugs, lighting, kitchenware and accessories.*

**DESIGNERS GUILD**
267-277 Kings Road
London SW3 5EN
+44 (0)20 7351 5775
Designersguild.com

*Slimline, neatly proportioned seating options including daybeds and modular sofas in trademark range of pale and contemporary bright linens, velvets, cottons and upholstery weaves. Also a coordinating range of bed/bath linens and home accessories.*

**HABITAT**
Habitat.co.uk

*Affordable mid-range compact and sectional seating, storage and contemporary accessories.*

**THE HOLDING COMPANY**
theholdingcompany.co.uk

*Huge selection of smart storage ideas from boxes, rails, hooks and units to versatile shelving systems and wardrobe organizers.*

**IKEA**
Ikea.com

*Great value basic home essentials, include furniture, textiles and accessories. Clever modular kitchens in classic and traditional styles with selection of different height and width units to fit compact spaces.*

**JOHN LEWIS**
Johnlewis.com

*Classic one-stop shop for quality household essentials, soft furnishings, own brand and designer homewares and kitchen appliances in compact sizes.*

**MUJI**
Muji.eu

*Affordable, practical and stylish Japanese basics and great storage with stores nationwide and throughout Europe.*

**PIMPERNEL AND PARTNERS**
Pimpernelandpartners.co.uk

*Charming online collection of small sofas and French antique and vintage indoor and garden furniture pieces in dainty shapes and styles.*

**SOFA.COM**
Sofa.com

*Sofas, loveseats and armchairs in compact shapes and sizes, and upholstered storage beds with versatile loose cover options.*

**UNTO THIS LAST**
230 Brick Lane
London E2 7EB
+44 (0)20 7613 0882
Untothislast.co.uk

*Birch ply super-slim furniture designs including tables, benches, shelving and storage ideal for compact spaces in range of size options.*

### KITCHENS

**BOSCH**
bosch-home.co.uk

*Quality engineering and design in extensive range of compact and slimline kitchen appliances.*

**PLAIN ENGLISH**
plainenglishdesign.co.uk

*UK and USA studio producing fine craftsmanship and clean-lined traditional-style custom-built kitchens and storage.*

### HOMEWARES AND ACCESSORIES

**BRICKETT DAVDA**
Brickettdavda.com

*Simple handmade tableware. Beautiful organic shaped plate-cum-bowls and multi-purpose vessels in landscape-inspired soft natural hues.*

**EGG**
Eggtrading.com

*Inspiring small gallery space selling a curated collection of ceramics and fashion with a minimalist aesthetic.*

**GARDEN TRADING**
Gardentrading.co.uk

*Stylish modern updates to utilitarian storage, kitchenware and household essentials.*

**HOLLOWAYS OF LUDLOW**
Hollowaysofludlow.com

*Extensive range of quality architectural ironmongery, period fittings and lighting for making a statement in a small interior.*

**ROCKETT ST GEORGE**
Rockettstgeorge.co.uk

*Quirky furniture and home accessories, ideal for adding personality to a tiny home. Great industrial-style storage pieces.*

**TOAST**
Toast.co.uk

Capsule collection of relaxed textiles, bed linens, ceramics, textiles and storage ideas with an artisan feel.

**THE WHITE COMPANY**
Thewhitecompany.com

Stores nationwide and USA selling all-white palette of elegant home furnishings, textiles and linens.

## PAINTS AND FABRICS

**CABBAGES AND ROSES**
121–123 Sydney Street
London SW3 6NR
+44 (0)20 7352 7333
Cabbagesandroses.com

Pretty, coordinated range of soft and subtle faded florals, ideal for adding elegance to a small home.

**THE CLOTH SHOP**
290 Portobello Road
London W10 5TE
+44 (0)20 8968 6001
Theclothshop.net

Fabrics emporium with wide selection of washed linens, Swedish linens, cotton prints, velvets and French mattress ticking as well as buttons, ribbons, braids and vintage household textiles.

**FARROW AND BALL**
Farrow-ball.com

Sublime paint colours with good selection of warm off-whites, and classic, hand-block wallpapers with small print designs.

**FIRED EARTH**
Firedearth.com

Wide range of paint colours, wallpapers and tiles in contemporary and classic designs for adding a style statement to a small interior.

**LIBERTY**
Regent Street
London W1B 5AH
+44 (0)20 7734 1234
Liberty.co.uk

Classic fabric print designs galore for soft furnishings. Extensive haberdashery and home ware department.

**THE RUG COMPANY**
+44 (0)20 3369 3912
therugcompany.com

Designer handmade contemporary and traditional style rugs and floor coverings in a selection of colours, patterns and sizes.

# USA

## FURNITURE AND STORAGE

**CRATE AND BARREL**
Crateandbarrel.com

Stores nationwide. One-stop affordable furniture and accessories. Wide range of compact sofa solutions and practical storage.

**DWELL STUDIO**
Dwellstudio.com

Sectional sofas plus benches and ottomans that work well in small spaces. Also decorative accessories.

**FURNI FIT**
furni-fit.com

Affordable custom-made furniture that's made to fit your space, including a dining table, desk and coffee table plus a storage cube and bookscase.

**KERF DESIGN**
Kerfdesign.com

Seattle-based custom furniture and cabinet shop offering a range of storage solutions and furniture options plus their own wall-mounted Kerf Wall storage system ideal for small spaces.

**IKEA**
Ikea.com

Great value small-space kitchens plus many compact storage systems.

**KETER**
Keter.com

Home storage systems including plastic boxes in every shape and size

**POTTERY BARN**
Potterybarn.com

Contemporary furniture and accessories and small space specifics. Online design guides covering compact decorating solutions.

**RESTORATION HARDWARE**
restorationhardware.com

Extensive collection of scaled down, smaller proportioned furniture pieces specifically for smaller spaces.

**STACKS AND STACKS**
stacksandstacks.com

Kitchen and home essentials and storage, organizing and furnishing solutions with boxes, crates and baskets for all sorts of uses.

**WEST ELM**
westelm.com

One stop shop for furniture and accessories. Versatile modular storage systems and design service with online inspiration section with solutions specific for compact living.

## HOMEWARES AND ACCESSORIES

**ANTHROPOLOGIE**
Anthropologie.com

Curated mix of bright, eclectic home decor and accessories for adding a dash of colour and style to a tiny space and selection of one off vintage pieces too.

**THE CONTAINER STORE**
Thecontainerstore.com

Practical and aesthetic storage solutions for all rooms including closet storage, kitchen tidies and shelving.

**JONATHAN ADLER**
Jonathanadler.com

Colourful graphic designs on everything from cushions to upholstery and ceramics.

## KITCHENS

**COMPACT APPLIANCE**
Compactappliance.com

Online store specializing in compact appliances for tight urban homes, including compact fridges, wash and dry combo washers and counter-size dishwashers.

**SUMMIT APPLIANCE**
Summitappliance.com

Compact refrigerators and freezers especially designed for hard-to-fit spaces.

# PICTURE CREDITS

**Front endpapers** The home of the stylist and writer Sara Emslie in London; **1-2** Designed by Stéphane Garotin and Pierre Emmanuel Martin of Maison Hand in Lyon; **3** Designed by Armando Elias and Hugo D'Enjoy of Craft Design; **4** The home of the stylist and writer Sara Emslie in London; **5** The Paris apartment of Thierry Dreano, designed by the architect Sylvie Cahen; **6** The home of the stylist and writer Sara Emslie in London; **7** Pauline's apartment in Paris, designed by Marianne Evennou www.marianne-evennou.com; **8-9** The seaside home of designer Marta Nowicka, available to rent; **10-11** The family home of architect Arash Nourinejad and artist Kristina Lykke Tønnesen in Copenhagen; **12** The home of Birgitte and Henrik Moller Kastrup in Denmark; **13** Pauline's apartment in Paris, designed by Marianne Evennou www.marianne-evennou.com; **14** The home of Grant and Sam, owners of Petite Violette in Malmö, Sweden; **15** The home of Birgitte and Henrik Moller Kastrup in Denmark; **16** *left* Saša Antić – Interior stylist, set and props; **17** The seaside home of designer Marta Nowicka, available to rent; **18** The Paris apartment of Thierry Dreano, designed by the architect Sylvie Cahen; **19** Pauline's apartment in Paris, designed by Marianne Evennou www.marianne-evennou.com; **20** *left* Anne Hubert designer of La Cerise sur le Gâteau www.lacerisesurlegateau.fr; **20-21** Pauline's apartment in Paris, designed by Marianne Evennou www.marianne-evennou.com; **22** The Paris apartment of Thierry Dreano, designed by the architect Sylvie Cahen; **23** Pauline's apartment in Paris, designed by Marianne Evennou www.marianne-evennou.com; **24** *left* The family home of architect Arash Nourinejad and artist Kristina Lykke Tønnesen in Copenhagen; **24** *centre* Anne Hubert designer of La Cerise sur le Gâteau, www.lacerisesurlegateau.fr; **24** *right* The Paris apartment of Thierry Dreano, designed by the architect Sylvie Cahen; **25** The home of Birgitte and Henrik Moller Kastrup in Denmark; **26-27** Designed by Armando Elias and Hugo D'Enjoy of Craft Design; **28** *left* Designed by Stéphane Garotin and Pierre Emmanuel Martin of Maison Hand in Lyon; **28** *right* Saša Antić – Interior stylist, set and props; **29** The home of the stylist and writer Sara Emslie in London; **30** Saša Antić – Interior stylist, set and props; **31** *above* The seaside home of designer Marta Nowicka, available to rent; **31** *below* Anne Hubert designer of La Cerise sur le Gâteau, www.lacerisesurlegateau.fr; **32** *left* The family home of architect Arash Nourinejad and artist Kristina Lykke Tønnesen in Copenhagen; **32** *right* The home of the stylist and writer Sara Emslie in London; **33** *above* Anne Hubert designer of La Cerise sur le Gâteau, www.lacerisesurlegateau.fr; **33** *below* Designed by Stéphane Garotin and Pierre Emmanuel Martin of Maison Hand i n Lyon; **34** Anne Hubert designer of La Cerise sur le Gâteau, www.lacerisesurlegateau.fr; **35** The family home of architect Arash Nourinejad and artist Kristina Lykke Tønnesen in Copenhagen; **36** *above* The home of Birgitte and Henrik Moller Kastrup in Denmark; **36** *below* The home of the stylist and writer Sara Emslie in London; **37** *above left* The Paris apartment of Thierry Dreano, designed by the architect Sylvie Cahen; **37** *above right* The seaside home of designer Marta Nowicka, available to rent; **37** *below right* The Paris apartment of Audrée Chabert, designed by the architect Sylvie Cahen; **38** The home of Grant and Sam, owners of Petite Violette in Malmö, Sweden; **39** *above left* The seaside home of designer Marta Nowicka, available to rent; **39** *above right* Designed by Stéphane Garotin and Pierre Emmanuel Martin of Maison Hand in Lyon; **39** *below left* The home of Birgitte and Henrik Moller Kastrup in Denmark; **39** *below right* The family home of architect Arash Nourinejad and artist Kristina Lykke Tønnesen in Copenhagen; **40** Saša Anti – Interior stylist, set and props; **41** *above* The seaside home of designer Marta Nowicka, available to rent; **41** *below* Designed by Stéphane Garotin and Pierre Emmanuel Martin of Maison Hand in Lyon; **42-43** Saša Antić – Interior stylist, set and props; **44-53** The home of the stylist and writer Sara Emslie in London; **54-61** Pauline's apartment in Paris, designed by Marianne Evennou www.marianne-evennou.com; **62-69** The home of Birgitte and Henrik Moller Kastrup in Denmark; **70-85** Designed by Stéphane Garotin and Pierre Emmanuel Martin of Maison Hand in Lyon; **86-93** The family home of architect Arash Nourinejad and artist Kristina Lykke Tønnesen in Copenhagen; **94-101** The Paris apartment of Thierry Dreano, designed by the architect Sylvie Cahen; **102-111** The home of Grant and Sam, owners of Petite Violette in Malmö, Sweden; **112-119** Saša Antić – Interior stylist, set and props; **120-129** Anne Hubert designer of La Cerise sur le Gâteau, www.lacerisesurlegateau.fr; **130-137** The Paris apartment of Audrée Chabert, designed by the architect Sylvie Cahen; **138-147** The seaside home of designer Marta Nowicka, available to rent; **148-155** Designed by Armando Elias and Hugo D'Enjoy of Craft Design; **160** Anne Hubert designer of La Cerise sur le Gâteau, www.lacerisesurlegateau.fr; **Back endpapers** The home of the stylist and writer Sara Emslie in London.

# BUSINESS CREDITS

## SAŠA ANTIĆ
www.sasaantic.com
sasaantic.tumblr.com

*Pages 16 left; 28 right; 30; 40; 42-43; 112-119.*

## SYLVIE CAHEN ARCHITECT
T: +33 (0)1 73 77 38 25
E: sc@sylviecahen.com
www.sylviecahen.com

*Pages 5; 18; 22; 24 right; 37 above left; 37 below right; 94-101; 130-137.*

## ARMANDO ELIAS AND HUGO D'ENJOY
Craft Design Co
E: info@craftdesign.co
www.craftdesign.co

*Pages 3; 26 27; 148-155.*

## SARA EMSLIE
www.saraemslie.com

*Endpapers; pages 4; 6; 29; 32 right; 36 below; 44-53.*

## MARIANNE EVENNOU
www.marianne-evennou.com

*Pages 7; 13; 19; 20-21; 23; 54-61.*

## STÉPHANE GAROTIN AND PIERRE EMMANUEL MARTIN
Maison Hand
E: info@maison-hand.fr
www.maison-hand.com

*Pages 1-2; 28 left; 33 below; 39 above right; 41 below; 70-85.*

## ANNE HUBERT
La Cerise sur le Gâteau
www.lacerisesurlegateau.fr

*Pages 20 left; 24 centre; 31 below; 33 above; 34; 120 129; 160.*

## ARASH NOURINEJAD
E: info@anour.dk
www.anour.dk

and

## KRISTINA LYKKE TØNNESEN
www.kristinalykke.dk

*Pages 10-11; 24 left; 32 left; 35; 39 below right; 86-93.*

## MARTA NOWICKA
www.martanowicka.com

*Pages 8-9; 17; 31 above; 37 above right; 39 above left; 41 above; 138-147.*

## PETITE VIOLETTE
Online shop, retail space and prop hire business

Davidshallstorg 1
211 45 Malmö
Sweden
T: +46 (0)709 487 929
E: info@petiteviolette.com
www.petiteviolette.com

*Pages 14; 38; 102-111.*

# INDEX

Page numbers in *italic* refer to the illustrations

**A**
antiques 36
apartments
   Copenhagen 86–93
   London 148–55
   Lyon 70–7, 78–85
   Malmö 102–11
   Paris 54–61, 94–101, 120–9, 130–7
   Stockholm 112–19
appliances 82, *85, 130*
architects 20
architectural features 12–15
attics 17, 53, *129,* 133, 140–2, *146*

**B**
basements 17
beach houses 62–9
beams 16, *61, 128, 131, 133, 134*
boats 8
books *91, 116–17, 129*
boxes, storage *90,* 91–2
Britain 44–53, 138–57
budgets 18–20

**C**
Cahen, Sylvie 133–7
caravans 8
ceiling heights 12, 17
cellars 17
children's rooms *92, 144*
chimneybreasts 17, *17,* 49
cladding 67, 76
clothes rails *129*
clutter 31
colour 32–5, 88–91, 117, 123–5, 134–7, 155
Copenhagen 86–93
cottages 16, 24, 138–57
cubes and pods 23, *154,* 155

curtains, as cupboard doors *39, 58,* 60, *60, 74*

**D**
dark colours 70–7, 123
Denmark 62–9, 86–93
designing small spaces 23–5
digital fabrication 153
displays *28–30,* 40–1, 53, *83, 85, 104, 115, 117–19,* 119, *122*
doors
   cantina-style *137*
   sliding *16,* 17, 68, *68, 110*
dual-purpose rooms 23, *52*

**E**
Eames, Charles *151*

**F**
finances 18–20
fireplaces 46, *48,* 49, *49*
floor plans 15
France 54–61, 70–7, 78–85, 94–101, 120–9, 130–7
Funen 62–9
furniture 36–7

**G**
glass walls *71,* 73–4, *73, 77*

**H**
hallways 56–7
headboards 36, 126, *126*

**I**
island, kitchen *106–7*

**L**
ladders *9, 144*
lateral living 16–17
light, natural 15, 32, 108, 123, 134

lighting 33, *75,* 76, *76, 126*
loft conversions 17
London 148–55
Lyon 70–7, 78–85

**M**
Malmö 102–11
mantelpieces *6*
mezzanine levels 17, 24, 57–9, *60–1, 63,* 64, 99, *100–1,* 106, 155, *155*
minimalism 31
mirrors 41, *41,* 81, *83, 85, 113,* 118

**N**
natural light 15, 32, 108, 123, 134

**O**
office spaces 18, *19, 53, 125, 154,* 155

**P**
Panton, Verner *151*
Paris 54–61, 94–101, 120–9, 130–7
partition walls *112, 114,* 117–18
pattern *32,* 35
period houses 16–17, 23–4
pictures *40,* 41, *118–19*
planning 18–21
plants *103*
plaster walls 142–5, *145*
plate racks *39,* 68
pods and cubes 23, *154,* 155
proportions 36, 125–6
Prouvé, Jean *151*

**R**
Race, Ernest *140*
radiators *20*
Richmond, Surrey 44–53

Riley, Bridget *138*
rugs 76

**S**
scale 36, 125–6
shutters *8,* 49–50
sleeping platforms *13*
Sluseholmen 86–93
space, sense of 12–15
stairs *9, 22,* 49, *56, 94, 144, 152,* 155
Stockholm 112–19
storage 24–5, *24–5,* 38–9, 91–2
summerhouses 62–9
Sussex 138–57
Sweden 102–11, 112–19

**T**
televisions *73*
terraced houses 24, 44–53, 138–57
textures 81
tiles 84
trolleys *102, 107*

**V**
Velux windows *132*
vertical living 16–17

**W**
walls
   cladding 67, 76
   displays 40, *40–1*
   glass walls *71,* 73–4, *73, 77*
   partition walls *112, 114,* 117–18
   plaster walls 142–5, *145*
washing machines 82, *85*
white 32–3, 50, 88, 100, 117, 123–5, 134–7
work spaces 18, *19, 53, 125, 154,* 155

**Z**
zoning areas 56

# ACKNOWLEDGMENTS

Thank you to everyone at Ryland Peters and Small for giving me the opportunity to produce this book. Especially to Annabel, who was an absolute pleasure to work with at every stage, to Leslie and Toni for such lovely art direction and layouts, and to Jess for getting all the locations rounded up and for our meticulously planned travel itineraries that got us everywhere we needed to go and home again! Thank you of course to Rachel for taking such fabulous photographs and for capturing the essence of each interior so perfectly.

A huge thank you also to all the homeowners for welcoming us to their homes and for sharing their own inspired thinking on small-space living.

Finally, thank you to my Dad for all his encouragement and seemingly limitless words of wisdom, not just for this but for always – I do listen!

This book is dedicated to the memory of my beautiful mum.